Get to Work...
on OUR Future

© 2019. ISDN: 9781704375823

To my son, Collin

This is for you, because of you.

You are my greatest accomplishment; you are my life. You are why I needed,
need to be better … why all of us ahead of you need to be better

… why you will need to be better for all those who are or will come behind you.

Please get to work on your and everyone else's future.

I love you.

Get to Work...
on OUR Future

Foreword

Michael Falk, CFA has written his second important book. The first one, *Let's All Learn How to Fish*, explored entitlement systems: retirement, healthcare, and education. In his thoughtful and carefully researched fashion, he offers solutions to these vexing societal issues. In this period of political polarization, in which the left and right can barely speak to one another, let alone do it in a constructive way, Michael offers nonpartisan ideas that bridge the gap. And make eminent sense.

Now, in this second book, he goes deeper, again using a tone that is fair and logical, and therefore appealing to both conservatives and liberals. An example from a social gathering comes to mind. Michael was at my family's house, chatting about his favorite topics—those covered in his books—when two guests with diametrically opposing views joined the conversation. I wondered how long it would be until the usual fireworks erupted. The faces of the two guests in question appeared to be bracing for battle. They were anchored in their positions and were ready to pounce. Michael continued talking calmly about various social issues like income distribution, healthcare, and retirement. His knowledge of the subjects and his clear devotion to fairness, responsibility, and economic well-being slowly disarmed the combatants. They relaxed and began to listen. His new book sums up his eminently agreeable approach with the guiding mantra of:

> *Let's choose this new ERA and lose our Entitled mentalities to*
> *take Responsibility and Appreciate those who need assistance.*

If you knew the combatants in the story above, you would appreciate the important contribution that Michael is making to the current political discussions in our world. How do we get beyond the emotional arguments that are raging on these topics and move towards calm and considered solutions? Topics that matter to us all.

Importantly, you should know a little about Michael. Does his life align with the messages in his books? Does he use his good mind to write about principles like fairness, responsibility, and appreciation but abandon them in practice? I have known Michael for many years, as a business partner and close friend, and I assure you that he is one of the most principled, fair-minded, and trustworthy people that I know. He is the guy who helps mothers-to-be put their luggage in the overhead compartment and surrenders his seat to senior citizens. He believes passionately that everyone deserves a fair chance at a good life. And his books provide a game plan.

I hope all policy makers read both of Michael's books and take them to heart. They are written in a clear, conversational style, unlike the unreadable tomes that come from politicians and academics. As you read this book and nod at the wisdom of his ideas, I hope you will recommend them to all your friends. And even more crucially to policy makers who wield influence. We all have responsibility. The world is crying out for real solutions. Michael provides them in this new book.

If the world is ready, Michael offers solutions. Ready or not, it's time.

Jim Ware, CFA,
Founder of the Focus Consulting Group,
Author of six books, consultant and speaker

My Warm-Up

Inequality is a real issue and a growing concern today. And, if the cries about "the robots are coming, the robots are coming" are realized, inequality could become much worse. We can't "afford" inequality today, much less if it grows worse. We need to address the issue, NOW. First and foremost, we need to agree on what we're discussing. What *inequality*? Income and wealth inequality are inarguable, so I prefer a different focus, on that which leads to those disparities: *opportunity inequality*. Let's strive for opportunity equality, which would offer more to everyone, everywhere, and for all time. In short, too many people lack a "fair shot." If a great many more get that fair shot, the likelihood of all of us benefiting from the next great thinker, designer, or leader increases due to the law of large numbers.[1] Equality of opportunity is also more inclusive, appreciative, and cohesive for a society.

Why did I bother to write this book? Because a fair shot requires that some perspectives (and policies) will have to change. It will require improved **governance** (Chapter 1); a healthier perspective on and about **work** (Chapter 2); a deeper understanding of what **robots will, won't**, and **might do** to us (Chapter 3); and greater clarity on what **income for everyone** could mean (Chapter 4). Now is the time for all of us to "Get to Work … on OUR Future!"

This expedition all began with my 2016 book *Let's All Learn How to Fish … To Sustain Long-Term Economic Growth*. There I dared to share my ideas about how to rethink entitlement policies such as those linked to retirement, healthcare, and education to promote and welcome sustainable economic growth. Those three policy topics are interconnected and happen to connect to society's biggest costs. The interconnection is as simple as this proposition: Retirement ages have to be raised to help sustain an economy, and for that to be possible people need to be healthy enough to work; possess the relevant skills to do work; and be able to find, maintain, retain, or create

---

[1] If you don't believe me, read Max Roser, "Talent is everywhere, opportunity is not. We are all losing out because of this," *Our World in Data* (Sept. 19, 2019), https://ourworldindata.org/talent-is-every-where-opportunity-is-not and wonder how many more Alberts and Maries we will all recognize!

jobs. Fixing any single one of these three elements is insufficient and would create other challenges; the three must be fixed in concert. My overarching goals were to (1) facilitate a better dialogue on topics that can be very personal and challenging, (2) raise the critical idea of opportunity equality, and (3) maybe—just maybe—help motivate many to rethink their own positions on these foundational policies. After dozens of speeches and fascinating Q&A sessions around the United States (as well as in 12 other countries) over the past few years, I began to wonder if the biggest entitlement might just be employment. "If I get an education, learn some skills, and am dependable, then someone *should* employ me and pay me X wages … that *should* be at least $Y." **Why?** And what happens when and if more jobs are lost due to external forces such greater automation and use of robots? More nationalism? Please, no!

Job losses due to automation and robots are a risk, but right now (2019) the U.S. unemployment rate, as measured, is the lowest it has been in decades. Good. But let's remain concerned about how many may have dropped out of the labor force and are no longer being counted. Countless individuals approached me after my speeches with genuine appreciation for some of my policy ideas (which meant more to me than you could have realized—thank you!), but they also asked how opportunity equality would work if there aren't enough jobs to go around. That's an interesting question/topic, and what motivated me to write this next and final part of what became known as my fishing expedition.

Now that my warm-up is complete, wish me luck for my start and for not too many wild pitches.

My Start

Did you know that if we took the 2017 U.S. gross domestic product (GDP) and divided it by the number of adults in the United States, we would get an estimated per capita income of roughly $56,000 per adult? Not for an entire family, *per adult*. Doing a similar exercise, but for hours worked, we see that the average adult works just three hours per day.[2] Now, just imagine what the average income or GDP could be if the actual work done stretched closer to the storied eight-hour workday. Still, averages such as the $56,000 and the three hours per day hide an awful lot of useful information. In fact, even though statistics can be worse than "damned lies,"[3] this "average" level of productivity is shockingly good. More to the point, if we consider that not everyone is always capable of producing at various times during their lives, such as during childhood or retirement, or if they're differently abled, then wouldn't, shouldn't, a high-minded society want to produce enough to support those less able as well as themselves? Certainly. So, let's all get to work on our future: a future that we all share.

It's important to keep in mind that although jobs come and go, there is never a fixed number of them, and the sheer number of them has continued to grow throughout history along with the population growth, keeping pace! Nevertheless, the growing success of robots and other automation technology has brought genuine fear regarding the availability of jobs. That fear includes the loss of work, the risk of less or lesser work (and income), and concerns about opportunity generally. Given those fears and the present disparity between the haves and have-nots, the topic of inequality deserves exploration and explanation—or at least some attention.

---

2   Jeff Sachs, economist, podcast on Oct. 16, 2018 @ 32:30. https://bankingthefuture.com/the-exponential-view-with-azeem-azhar/?utm_source=The+Financial+Revolutionist+Weekly+Briefing&utm_campaign=d2e5d06cc9-EMAIL_CAMPAIGN_2018_10_19_10_14_COPY_01&utm_medium=email&utm_term=0_bbba91202b-d2e5d06cc9-77261149&mc_cid=d2e5d06cc9&mc_eid=379022604e

3   "There are three kinds of lies: lies, damned lies, and statistics." This saying has been attributed to Mark Twain as well as several others.

Is inequality simply probabilistic—a risk—within a population of people or is it a bit evil on the part of the winners?[4] Successful people have become demonized in many parts of the media for their striving and "winning." While some of today's inequality levels can seem a bit evil, consider that inequality may simply be a fact of life. We're each biologically endowed with mental and physical attributes from birth in our genes (apart from all other possible endowments); this is inequality and it's 100% natural. There are also very unequal drivers and factors, such as where you grew up, when you grew up, and much more.[5] Let's appreciate our diversity, and instead question whether individual and unequal beginnings should be able to affect our lives, and if so, to what extent. Consider this economist's perspective:[6]

> As a thought experiment, let us imagine that with today's powerful computers it was possible to design a centrally planned economic system that could achieve an output level twice as high as an imperfect, unstable free-market system. And, now let's imagine that the wealth of this centrally planned system is divided equally amongst the workers along communist lines. What would the likely response be to this fixed reward system, if we really are naturally competitive?

> As we could not compete on the output of the system—that is, the rewards—we would naturally start to compete on the inputs, the work. The only way to gain a competitive upper hand relative to our peers would be to receive the same fixed benefit for a lower amount of work. In this way we would at least enjoy a greater benefit per unit of work. Of course, the result would be a race to the bottom, with everyone competing to do less than each other—we call this demotivation—until management, or the politburo, resorted to coercion … If we are really Darwinian competitors, we must accept an uneven distribution of rewards as the cost of maintaining motivation.[7]

An uneven distribution of rewards has real and necessary benefits. Agreed. My argument is simply that the *opportunity* to reap rewards should be equal.

---

4 It could also be asked whether the losers' feeding off of the winners, rather than trying to win themselves, is evil. However, that type of view presupposes that each person has sufficient opportunities to win.

5 I addressed this topic in chapter 2 of my prior book, *Let's All Learn to Fish*; in short, I probably grew up at least on third base so that scoring would be just one "sacrifice" (bunt or fly ball) away for me (hello to my fellow baseball fans).

6 For those who don't like economists, consider that "[a]ll progress comes from the creative minority … If our government continues to smear, harass, overtax, and oppressively regulate them, we will be dismayed by how swiftly the engines of American prosperity deteriorate. We will be amazed at how quickly American wealth flees to other countries." These words are from campaign speeches of former President Barack Obama.

7 George Cooper, *Fixing Economics* (Harriman House, 2016), p. 134.

Should there also be a limit to the amount of the unequal distributions? If so, what should that amount be? First, I think that any limits are arguably unsustainable and would be arbitrary. Second, limits are a bad idea. If big producers are limited, then overall production could fall. Remember that misleading average $56,000 statistic: it's misleading because of the disproportionately large incomes that increase it; the middle (median) income is less than $40,000. The permitted-disparity question may also be made moot if opportunity equality exists and a minimal platform from which to launch into adulthood is provided to everyone. Let's ensure opportunity equality and consider how we might construct that platform. There are a couple of questions to keep in mind.

How much "stuff" might never have been created or imagined without an income motivation? Creation/invention/production is the result of an income motivation (among others) that allows just three hours of work to produce a per capita adult income of roughly $56,000.

Is wealth inequality different from income inequality, and if so, how? Maybe there's no difference if we think of wealth as being the result of accumulated, invested income. (For now, let's exclude inheritances.) Wealth inequality could be managed through charitable tax incentives and estate or wealth taxes. Keep in mind that *real* wealth grows over time through compounding and ownership, independent from work efforts. Since both income and wealth are desired by most people, we must try to be very constructive when setting tax policy to avoid any incentives to stop working. *Constructive* is a "nice" term that is intended to capture opportunity equality along with simultaneously preserving income motivations. Put simply, **(1) people need to be able to GET IN the game; (2) the game should have clear, understandable RULES applied EQUALLY to all the players; and (3) the game should offer EQUAL OPPORTUNITIES to win or lose.** Fair inequality[8] does work for people. Maybe we should just make a little itty-bitty addition to the fair inequality research: "as long as losing isn't punitive?"

What about George Cooper's "lower amount of work … demotivation?" Today, we may have gone beyond Cooper's well-founded fear with all our well-intentioned safety nets. Many nets have captured (seduced?) some people and are essentially keeping them down.[9] From my global audiences, I can attest to the fact that there are people who think the original design of these nets was not well-intentioned at all, but rather stitched together to keep/hold certain people down. If that's true … ugh! Of course,

---

8   Christina Starmans, Mark Sheskin, and Paul Bloom, "Why people prefer unequal societies," *Nature Human Behaviour* 1, art. no. 0082 (2017).

9   In *Let's All Learn to Fish*, I stated that we need nets for those unable/incapable and trampolines for everyone else.

we could also be experiencing the unintended consequences of good intentions. Regardless of the original motivation(s), which we cannot know, today's safety nets have bolstered some entitlement mentalities such as "I *deserve* this" or "I *should* receive that." The challenge for all of us is that regardless of the intentions, the biggest U.S. safety nets, such as Social Security, Medicare, and Medicaid, are no longer strong enough for today's population in their current forms, based on the numbers of people either in or near poverty—and we can't sustainably afford them. Most importantly, the nets are not being refashioned. Why? In a word, we have the *politicians* we deserve (and their pandering political performances based on [influential/wealthy] constituents' cries).

We need a new "ERA" mindset: one that has evolved from today's **Entitled** mentalities to one of taking **Responsibility** with **Appreciation** for those unable to/incapable of being responsible, as argued in my first book. We need people to be productive: as much as possible, as many of them as possible, as skilled as the economy needs them to be, and as healthy/fit as possible to be able to undertake the task(s) at hand. We need all of us to play to the best of our abilities.

Let's All Learn to Fish shared perspectives on working populations (labor forces), working longer (retirement and healthcare), and working better (education), but I would like to briefly expand on those points as they pertain to the United States today. (Please note, though, that many elements will be relevant to others around the world as well.)

More labor: inputs are needed in our society

Figure 1. Labor Force Participation Rate

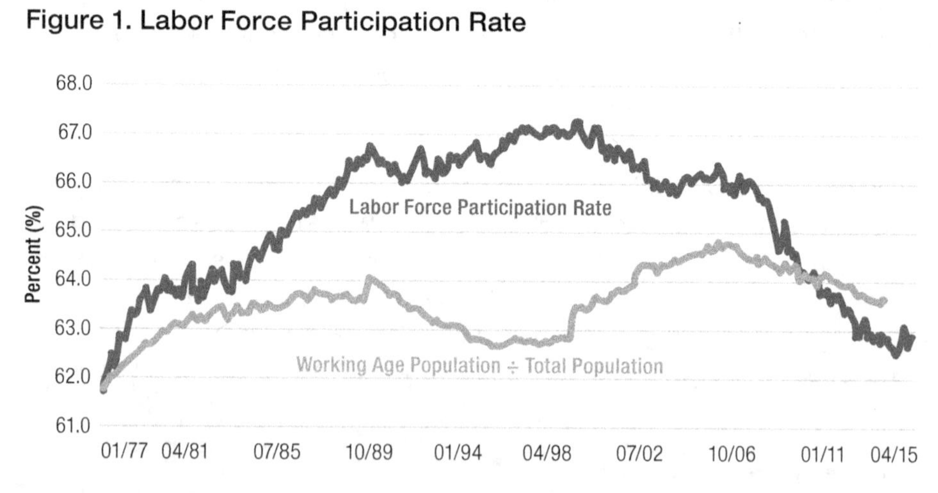

Source: Bureau of Labor Statistics, Federal Reserve Bank of St. Louis.

Labor has to be able to leap various employment hurdles. It is challenging by itself without any additional, artificial hills to climb (see Figure 1). To highlight two hills that seemingly don't have to be that way: people from outside of the United States who are denied entry yet are available, capable, and willing to join our labor force; and people who have aptitude but have their capabilities blocked.

Availability denied

Repeat after me: Immigrants do not take anyone's job and often take jobs that are less desirable or beyond a citizen's qualifications. A job "owed" is an entitlement mentality. If you think an immigrant took your job, please ask yourself: Why and how did they take it? Did you compete for it? Did they have a family to support, like you? Were they willing to work for less, be on time, show up every day? Did they have any unique qualifications?

Did you know that immigrants have historically come to the United States to work hard and better their own situations? This is the essence of an anti-entitlement sentiment. "Migration has also made America the innovation hub of the world. Immigrants are twice as likely as natives to start a company; more than 40% of the Fortune 500 were founded either by an immigrant or the child of one. Newcomers bring skills, connections and new ways of thinking." By that description, they bring jobs too. It's that very productivity boost that helps us all. Also, how do you react to the research findings showing that immigrants *lower* unemployment, when the immigration is job-related?[11] There's no denying that in aggregate immigration is a very good thing. Regardless, it could make sense to have an annual limit[12] on the number of immigrants allowed into the United States, to enable the economy to absorb the additional labor potential.

Other than based on a feeling of entitlement (or xenophobia, a/k/a bigotry), you cannot deny that more immigration is better than less immigration, if only to help offset the low (and falling) U.S. fertility rates. However, U.S. immigration policy (or its lack thereof) is badly in need of clarity, consistency, completeness, and quality (improvements). A policy should offer a path to citizenship and not be overcomplicated or burdensome to either current or future would-be citizens. Let's welcome their productivity. Could a sound policy be as simple as my plan below? First, consider the following table-stake policy thoughts:

---

10 "Governments need better ways to manage migration," *Economist* (Aug. 25, 2018).

11 Francesco Furlanetto and Ørjan Robstad, "Immigration and the macroeconomy: Some new empirical evidence," *VOX* (Dec. 10, 2016). https://voxeu.org/article/immigration-and-macroeconomy

12 A limit, instead of being an arbitrary number, could be linked to surveys of business needs or the U.S. fertility rate, as too few babies implies future labor shortages. Due to the time mismatch, if linked to the fertility rate, the linkage should consider immigrants' ages and prior years' fertility rates.

- No taxpayer-funded "safety net" help (e.g., worker's compensation, healthcare coverage, etc.) of any kind would be available prior to a person's becoming a citizen. Private employers, private citizens, or charitable organizations could offer help at their discretion via contributions into a local fund available for immigrants' use. The immigrants themselves might also be willing to contribute to help self-insure other immigrants in a form of "paying it forward."
- All arrivals into the United States would require biometric-style documentation such as fingerprints, blood types, and retinal scans to go along with the traditional name-and-address background type of information. All individuals would be allowed to enter the United States except for confirmed felons or those on intelligence watch lists. Inclusive, yes, but not careless. As an aside, we should all want better identification than a Social Security number, given the identity-theft risks that come along with such dated and nonsecure identifiers.
- Immigrants should learn to speak, read, and write the predominant local language (English in the United States) at a predetermined minimum level of competency to become a citizen. The value of a common language to greater societal cohesion cannot be overstated.
- Should there be an annual limit, if only to allow those who do come time to become incorporated into the fabric of this country?

Offers of citizenship (simple as 1-2-3)

1. Those with advanced degrees (master's level or higher) from a U.S. college will receive an offer to become citizens upon graduation; the offer of citizenship will be valid for 12 months following graduation.
2. An advanced or streamlined path would be available for those with verifiable university degrees or accreditation, from outside the United States, that can help meet business/employment needs. These individuals would receive "fast-tracked" citizenship, within 24 months.
3. For all others, the ability to become a citizen would be required to be achieved within 36 months of their arrival to the United States. If not, then they would have to leave the country no later than month 37. All current, noncitizen immigrants as of dd/mm/yyyy date would receive temporary amnesty but would need to achieve citizenship within this 36-month time period, effective upon enactment of the new regulation.

Children from birth to age 18 would be covered under their parent's citizenship status. No other relatives would be allowed to be linked in such a way. Young adults over the age of 18, or upon reaching age 18, would need to establish their own citizenship based on one of the 12-, 24-, or 36-month offers.

Aptitude "blocked"

Got a felony drug conviction? Good luck getting hired for a job. Felons don't often receive job opportunities, even though drug convictions rarely involve violent crimes. And, given the overly imprisoned U.S. population, along with the fact that it consists of so many minority prisoners (contributed to by stark opportunity inequality), drug abuse and drug-related convictions are limiting both the size and diversity of the overall labor force. Opioid abuse—which has reached epidemic status—is a special case of aptitude blocked. Regardless of whether opioid use causes disability or is the result of a prescription for disability, the destructive and addictive properties of real and synthetic opioids are the same. Worse yet, you can choose to include the word "predatory" when talking about opioids, due to the improper behaviors of some doctors, drug distributors and drug manufacturers who are being sued for their actions[13] and in some cases settling out of court (as of 2019).

Better labor is needed, and it need not require high IQs

This topic directly involves schooling/learning of so-called "people skills" such as collaboration and leadership. It begins early with supportive interventions and schooling for young children. Research has even shown the value of participation in a program that begins as early as 8 weeks of age and continues until age 5 and includes health screenings and food. The research population of 8-weeks- to 5-year-old children (who were followed until they turned age 35) showed a return of 13% per year to society over the 30-year period (Figure 2). This is a remarkable return on the investment, and is due to many factors, including avoidance of the criminal justice system (i.e., courts and jails) as these individuals grew up.

Figure 2. Returns to a unit dollar invested are highest in earliest years

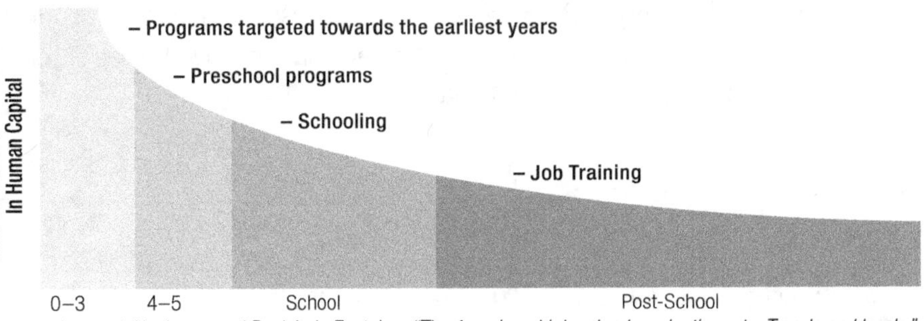

Source: James J. Heckman and Paul A. LaFontaine, "The American high school graduation rate: Trends and levels," NBER Working Paper Series no. 13670 (2007), http://www.nber.org/papers/w13670.

---

[13] Beth Mole, "DEA Tracked Every Opioid Pill Sold in the U.S." *Ars Technica* (July 7, 2019), https://arstechnica.com/science/2019/07/76-billion-opioid-pills-in-7-years-how-pharma-companies-drowned-us-in-drugs/

For those who thought or are still thinking that intervention as early as eight weeks seems nuts, even if possible, there's a program[14] that has shown real success with an approach for 4-year-olds in their own homes, the year before kindergarten. More on this topic in chapter 2 (except how family structures can help or hinder child development).

Labor for longer … as in a percentage of one's life
This topic is about promoting delayed retirements. After all, living longer without working for longer means a longer period of retirement. Except for the very few cases of those capable of financing their own retirement, retirement needs will grow, and will be shouldered by the shrinking labor force (based on the low/falling fertility rates around the world) as retirees are unable to finance their own retirement. And, yes, fertility rates around the world do affect the United States—fewer potential, future immigrants.

While we could enforce a policy of zero financial assistance prior to an older retirement age to help "incentivize" people to work longer, let's NOT. We should consider a more compassionate approach and set two retirement ages[15]: one for "blue-collar" workers (e.g., age 65) and an older age for "white-collar workers" (e.g., age 70) that better aligns people's physical capabilities with work requirements. Because Social Security and Medicare loom so large in most retirees' plans, incentives to work longer around these two entitlements are both influential and the easiest (at least in theory) to implement (if you don't count political risk).

What if we begin by taking one step toward removing the real or perceived costs of working later in life, by offering a disincentive to retire? Upon reaching the current Social Security full retirement age or Medicare's age 65,[16] people could be considered paid-up; there would be no more payroll taxes for them or their employers for their continued work.[17] Such an elegant incentive for both employer and employee is one that seems workable and not very expensive, either! Just as Social Security (essentially) pays many people to stop working who would otherwise remain *in* the labor force, this approach would make it pay to stay in the labor force.

---

[14] https://www.audaciousproject.org/ideas/2019/upstart-project

[15] In *Let's All Learn to Fish*, I advocated for this policy and two retirement ages, and discussed how to prevent people from gaming such a system.

[16] These "full" ages should be the same; I struggle to understand any current argument as to why they should be different.

[17] John Shoven (Stanford) & Robert Clark (UNC), "Enhancing work incentives for older workers: Social Security and Medicare proposals to reduce work disincentives" (Dec. 2, 2018), https://www.brookings.edu/wp-content/uploads/2018/12/2-Clark-Shoven.pdf

Other taxes

The research on saving payroll taxes is just one example of the power of taxation on behavior. Taxation is among the biggest of all financial incentives. Let's tax both constructively and inoffensively to encourage productivity, promote taking responsibility, and enable us to afford our necessary appreciations for those unable to work (be responsible). Although I put forth simplified (elegant?) tax ideas in *Let's All Learn to Fish*—that I still support—as effective and workable, I think it may be helpful to add a couple of new tax perspectives related to the topic of inequality.

Land

Land is arguably the oldest and among the most valuable of all entitlements (since it's often handed down). There's no more land being created, demand increases based on rising populations, and ownership of valuable land often exists for decades (or longer). Consider these historical perspectives:

- U.S. founding father, John Adams, said: "Power always follows property."
- The U.S. Declaration of Independence promotes "life, liberty, and the pursuit of happiness" and has been linked to John Locke's "life, liberty and property." Keep in mind that in the founding era, land use was primarily agrarian (used for farming), and control of your own land meant freedom.

Might we tax land? The idea of land taxes dates to 1879 (Henry George), but how might we pursue such a tax in modern times? Nobel Laureate Maurice Allais supported land taxes through an approach known as the "Harberger tax." This tax, named after economist Arnold Harberger, tries to balance private and societal ownership to increase everyone's welfare by ensuring that property is more productively utilized. (Think no vacant lots in New York City.) With the Harberger tax, owners would publicly declare (e.g., in a for-sale real estate database) the price at which they would be willing to sell their property; that's the value to be taxed. If owners declare too low a value, they will risk having the property bought. The simplicity and beauty of this tax approach cannot be overstated, and it's better enabled with today's technology.

However, the Harberger tax is a genuine risk to owners, and the frictional costs of property sales (such as the time it takes to ready a sale and transaction fees) make me wonder if there's another, better way that could work. What if the tax is based on something like the average monthly population density of the square mile that

---

[18] But let's recognize and appreciate how corporations organize labor in societies. They "leverage" the diverse work of many, and we all benefit from supporting them with low (but *not* no) taxes. As you will read later in this book, we could also count on them more to help prepare/train labor for work if we made better use of their tax payments.

surrounds the property (or some other standardized distance) for the past 12 months, rather than on a sale price? Consider a property in New York City versus land outside a small town in Wyoming. The productivity and opportunity costs of underdeveloped land in New York are much higher. To prevent land "squatters" from simply dumping their property at the inception of a Harberger tax, the seller could be obligated to carry the tax liability forward for a defined period after the sale or until a completed redevelopment of the property. The continuation of the tax could be capped from the sale unless the population density drops more than 10%, at which point the tax would be reduced ratably.

If used as a commercial (recommended) rather than a residential land (property) tax, such a tax could be added to any minimum corporate tax liability incurred by a business.[18] Consideration should be given to the business's expected longevity; for example, local bars and restaurants less than 5 years old may be exempt from the tax—until they reach 5 years of operation—whereas franchises/chains would be taxed immediately.

Wealth

Like land taxes, the concept of wealth taxes is not new. In fact, some countries have tried and scrapped wealth taxes. The idea of a wealth tax is being floated in 2019 due to the growing inequality levels and the increasing voices of some far-left politicians. Regardless, might inherited wealth be considered an entitlement? An interesting aspect of taxing wealth is that while income is a primary motivation to work, wealth is more like a success scorecard for those in the higher tiers of society (e.g., the top 0.5% or 0.1%). With taxes being such big incentives, we need to be very careful here, because society can't afford for our big "winners" to stop competing/winning.

What if a wealth tax were set at the marginal wealth threshold of the top 0.1% in society[19] (estimated at $32 million in 2019), and the tax was 1% on all wealth above that level? We can wonder:

- How such a tax may *not* interfere with entrepreneurial/success incentives, since at that arguably unspendable level of wealth (apart from "things" like multiple homes and private airplanes) work is often about a passion or special aptitude for that work rather than being motivated by the income. For those who are no longer working, it's still unspendable.

---

19 Steve Wamhoff, "The U.S. needs a federal wealth tax," *ITEP Report* (Jan. 2019).

- How such a tax could even motivate spending by these über-wealthy individuals prior to their reaching the taxable threshold, if they wished to avoid the tax, which would assist with economic or charitable growth.
- How the tax proceeds could benefit society—the estimates range from $1.3 to $2.7 trillion over a decade and dwarf the estate-tax proceeds that could be invested back into society. Those figures are based on taxing the 0.1%. If the threshold were dropped to the top 0.2% or 0.5%, the proceeds would be even larger, but keep in mind that there's a difference between what many might consider real wealth versus "hard-to-spend" wealth. One topic, Universal Basic Income (UBI; see chapter 4), has garnered some respect among both Democrats and Republicans, and is equally criticized due to its predicted costs and impact on work incentives. Might a wealth tax be a helpful funding mechanism and less of a negative incentive, since it's a direct response to inequality? Remember Bill Gates's "Giving Pledge," promoted to the world's billionaires, and how positively it has been received, on balance? Might a "giving" wealth tax that's spent strategically to alleviate inequality be received positively too? I can't help thinking that such a tax could be put to good use and even sequestered from the government's "general spending" to make it more acceptable to almost everyone, for all times.

The challenges with applying a wealth tax are real: it could require taxing authorities to know more about taxpayers than they currently do, and there's the difficulty with valuing less-liquid assets and the potential risks when selling such assets. However, I do think these difficulties can be overcome. For example, valuation challenges such as these are ripe for a Harberger-style tax assessment approach. And, while I would never recommend or want a tax that forces selling, owners could always sell down assets or shares in properties as their value grows, apart from many other techniques available to create enough money to pay the tax.

One last, mathematical perspective may be of interest. An annual wealth tax rather than an end-of-life estate tax would increase the compounding of wealth over time because the tax would be collected earlier and would directly reduce wealth inequality over time—aside from the taxes alone—to the extent that wealth inequality is the greatest concern.

---

[20] Governments borrowing to plug deficits is acceptable; borrowing for consumption is much less good than borrowing for investment purposes. The latter can bring long-term gains, whereas the former offers only debt payments for things consumed in the past. For example, during 2008–2009, the U.S. Treasury could have issued 50- or 100-year bonds. It didn't—UGH! Those bonds would have been gobbled up by global investors, providing cheap long-term financing for the U.S. government. What's more, the proceeds could have been used for infrastructure projects like fixing bridges or building out 5G capabilities that would have provided a great many jobs and promoted long-term U.S. growth.

I wrote *Let's All Learn How to Fish… To Sustain Long-Term Economic Growth* (2016) to initiate a proper dialogue, to argue for a change to today's "ERA," and to push for opportunity equality. However, I recognize that even with my rethought incentives—safety nets and trampolines (the core of that earlier book)—jobs are not guaranteed. Maybe after learning how to fish, we all need to begin fishing for jobs. Better yet, because a job comes from someone else and can be regarded as a form of entitlement, or at least a rigid structure to help work get done, let's reframe what we *want* as work—something most all of us can do on our own. So, let's get to work on our future, now that you have learned how to fish (or could) and end my 2016 "fishing expedition".

For a free PDF of my 2016 book, go to https://www.cfainstitute.org/en/research/foundation/2016/lets-all-learn-how-to-fish----to-sustain-long-term-economic-growth

It's also available as a free Kindle download: https://www.amazon.com/Learn-Sustain-Long-Term-Economic-Growth-ebook/dp/B01HMURMBA/ref=sr_1_1?keywords=lets+all+learn+how+to+fish&qid=1570908285&sr=8-1

Chapter 1: Governance

"When the people find that they can vote themselves money, that will herald the end of the republic."

—Benjamin Franklin

f the game should have clear rules that apply equally to all players, so as to offer a fair shot, then the topic of governance must be addressed.[21] This also involves how the rules are made in the first place. How individuals become elected officials, who both make the rules (laws) and officiate/referee the "game," plays a critical role. To avoid Franklin's "end of the republic," we need to balance the potential tyranny of self-interest with the democratic needs and benefits of social cohesion through fair governance and proper incentives. Apologies to Adam Smith and his invisible hand, but each of us acting selfishly, in our own interest, puts us on an unsustainable path due to the practice and amount of crony capitalism[22] or regulatory capture by those in power. Put simply, too many people can be slapped down by Smith's invisible hand.

We don't need to look any further than how polarized the U.S. government and the Democratic and Republican parties have become. Each party has been pursuing its own self-identified interests at the expense of social cohesion and the pursuit of grabbing/retaining control wherever possible. Capitalism need not be replaced—and it would be a serious mistake to do so—but it very much needs improved, unbiased officiating. Rules have to be applied equally, to everyone. And, while socialism's free

---

[21] With respect to the global orientation of my earlier book and this current one, please know that this chapter is biased toward the United States government's structure, but its principles hold for the world.

[22] Capitalism is much maligned, but I would argue that we are not playing the game with consistent and equal rules for everyone. Crony capitalism has created a bit of a club, money-influenced and able to perpetuate itself to a significant extent.

stuff is seductive, it's not so much free, but rather stuff paid for by others. It's capitalism that motivates the production of all that stuff in the first place.

Perhaps the most direct way to avoid Franklin's fear would be to limit who can influence the game's rulemaking and enforcement: that is, who can vote. *What if* the right to vote had to be earned (current constitutional limits aside)? More specifically, what if voting privileges were earned by citizens who pay federal or state income taxes? If votes had to be "earned" in this way, then at least there would be some payment for all the "free" stuff. The risk of those who receive the benefits of free stuff voting themselves more at zero cost to themselves is real and growing, and it could be largely undone with this single change in the rules. While this might seem *highly* undemocratic or just plain wrong, please recall the famous phrase "taxes are the price we pay for civilized society"[23]: why should society ever be discounted because some don't think they should have to pay? Regardless, there should always be an ability to "buy back" one's vote even if individuals have no tax liability. What if such a buyback was based on median income levels, and the vote cost the lesser of 2% of the federal/state median household income or $1,000, whichever is less, and payable through filing one's taxes?[24] No tax filing(s) or payment ... no vote. Might this beget more tax filings, hmm? What if any and all vote-payment proceeds were applied to repay federal and state debts directly? After all, aren't those debts largely attributable to entitlement programs? Although these funds could be used to help extinguish federal or state debts (please stop laughing[25]), we could be better off if those payment proceeds were to go toward local schools or facilities to support the greatest leveler for opportunity equality—child well-being—in the following priority order:

- Preschool (including one meal, or two if need be) would be available at no cost
- Full-day kindergarten (including breakfast and lunch) would be available at no cost
- Childcare (including one meal, or two if need be) would be available at no cost

Dedicating vote payments to these priorities would likely not cover the complete costs of effective preschool and kindergarten programs, but they would certainly lessen the impact of what should become societal requirements wherever they are not already. Why these requirements vary from place to place is an example of opportunity inequality

---

[23] U.S. Supreme Court Justice Oliver Wendell Holmes, Jr. (1927).

[24] An alternative to buying back the right to vote could be to value votes differently for those paying zero federal or state taxes. If less than age 35 or more than age 70 with zero taxes due, then your vote would count 50%.

[25] For modern monetary theorist (MMT) fans who may read this book, this is for you. I do not think MMT is safe, because of its dependence on sound, timely fiscal policy decisions (which seem to be rare events) and the continued privilege of the United States being the global reserve currency.

and makes it worse. Let's provide a massive boost to opportunity equality and its long-term benefits for society, and respect that these are child-related *investments* rather than expenditures.

If the "who can vote" is clear, then what about the "how we vote"? There are issues at both the federal and state levels with our how's.

Just say "no" to either/or voting

The current "pick one" voting approach practically guarantees the ongoing dominance of the two-party system. Consider that a third-party candidate is generally thought of as "stealing" votes from one of the two major parties' candidates, damaging the major-party candidate's electability and risking a winner by default. In the United States, this has made the viability of a third-party candidate all but impossible and is viewed very negatively by the most similar "other" candidate. This has the effect of limiting voter choice. Do you see this as a form of crony capitalism? The Democratic and Republican parties essentially "own" the path to major offices. Furthermore, they direct (contort?) the path toward their greatest likelihood of winning the office through registration and districting (boundary) games.

The issues with either/or voting can be mostly corrected with using what's called ranked choice voting (RCV).[26] RCV helps elect the most preferred candidate when there are three or more candidates by asking for the three to be ranked (for example, 1-2-3 or 3-1-2). This approach helps overcome the current polarization of the two-party system (Democrat and Republican) and allows for a potential third—more centrist (today)—candidate. Do most voters have what they think is real choice today? Hmm, maybe not. RCV would enable real choice and perhaps even help decrease party polarization while increasing the inclusiveness of voting.

How we register to vote, and cast our votes, must change. C'mon, it's the 21st century and we're still using paper? Really? If you vote, then your registration—which exists in the local census—should be contingent on your being a citizen and having an address that can be confirmed in public records and should be counted based on a biometric validation. All votes should be done electronically and "tallied" at that specific time of entry. The risks of registration problems, voter fraud, and missing ballots must and can end. The thought behind tallying votes immediately would reduce counting errors, missing vote errors, and the ability to tamper with votes, as well as creating a time- and place-stamped "fingerprint" to double-check a voter's selection(s) if need be.

---

26 https://www.fairvote.org/rcv#how_rcv_works

Let's graduate beyond the U.S. Electoral College

Shouldn't winning a federal election be decided by the citizenry and not where they live? With the current Electoral College requirements for election, locations and parties take on greater importance. The Electoral College may have[27] (or not?) served the United States well in the past, but it has failed us more recently. The popular vote hasn't elected the U.S. president for two of the past five elections. Should we simply have a popular, national vote? Maybe not, since that could cause less populous areas or even states to be ignored by candidates.

What if we required U.S. presidents (and state governors, too) to win popular, RCV votes per state? Furthermore, each state's RCV should be tallied across each of three distinct age cohorts: less than 35, 35 to 70, over 70. These three age cohorts are meant to simulate school and starting out, the primary work years, and in or near retirement (and should evolve over time as our life expectancies and corresponding policies shift). It would take a simple majority of any two out of the three cohorts to win a state and elect the governor, while the simple majority among all the states would determine who would be the next president. The two-out-of-three, simple majority is the key to avoiding the risk of Franklin's worries and the domination of any single either large or voting-age cohort. In particular, the working-age (35–70) cohort's productivity has primary responsibility for the support of both those younger and those older. However, the size of this cohort is declining as a share of the world population. This implies a potential need for (ever) more taxation of the working-age cohort and/or the imperative to extend what working age means, so we *desperately* need to consider how to maintain this group's motivation to work. Think: With fewer babies being born and improved longevity, a static retirement age (as in not aging as we age) means that the percentage of working people will continue to shrink relative to those who are retired (Figure 3) … assuming that immigration patterns hold (hmm).

---

[27] It served in the past by requiring the 270 EC votes and incentivizing candidates to visit many states and locations.

Figure 3. U.S. labor force growth will remain low for the foreseeable future

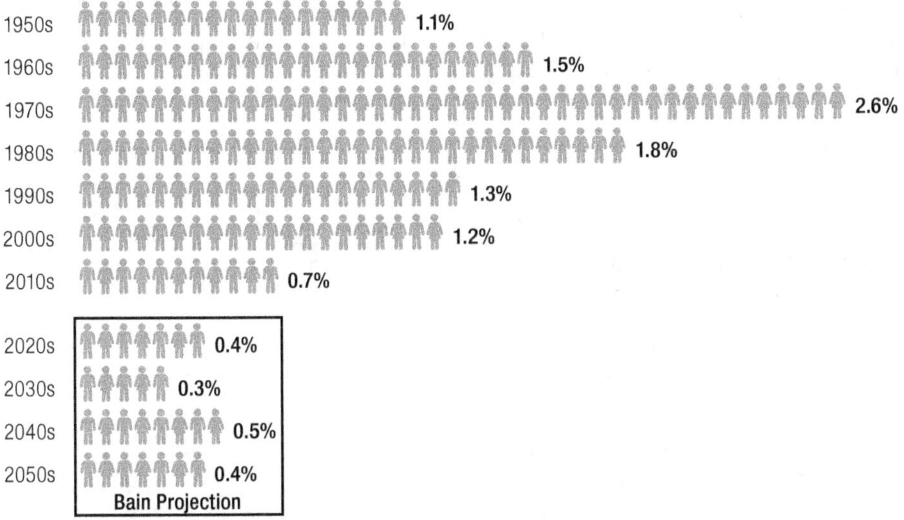

Source: U.S. Bureau of Labor Statistics, U.S. Census Bureau; Bain Macro Trends Group analysis (2017), https://www.bain.com/insights/labor-2030-the-collision-of-demographics-automation-and-inequality/

The intergenerational element of social contracts will come under ever more serious strain (than it is already), and this has major political ramifications based on evidence from other countries that are older than the United States. Consider that for every additional year in the age of the median voter in OECD countries, spending on pensions increases by 0.5% of GDP (out of 2% to 3% annual growth rates, this is big): a clear measure that older citizens are effective at influencing policy.[28] "Consider the UK (alone), where public spending on the elderly exceeds that spent on children, arguably because old people vote, and children do not."[29] I understand the need—in some cases—for being self-interested; however, generational narcissism is not good for sustaining society. And, yes, I acknowledge my use of harsh rhetoric; it grows out of the goal of asking an important question that begs for a societal answer. Recognize that for all the cries about democracy—worthwhile cries, in my opinion—the turnout of those who are eligible to vote in the U.S. presidential election is generally only around 60%, and only some 87% of those who are registered to vote.

---

[28] Friedrich Breyer and Ben Craig, "Voting on Social Security: Evidence from OECD countries," *European Journal of Political Economy* 13(4), 705–724 (1997).

[29] "Beveridge 2.0: Rethinking the welfare state for the 21st century": panel presentation by Dame Minouche Shafik, Director, London School of Economics (Nov. 29, 2017), http://www.lse.ac.uk/Events/2017/11/20171129t1830vLSE/beveridge

Could you ever imagine individuals above the retirement age not being allowed to vote? What happens when the working-age cohort is the minority? It's possible. A simple majority (two out of the three) across the distinct age cohorts would both continue to allow retired people to vote and yet lessen their ability to direct the vote for their own needs. We should never forget that it's restraints on majorities that are needed to protect minorities. I think Martin Niemöller said it best:

> First, they came for the socialists, and I did not speak out—because I was not a socialist.

> Then they came for the trade unionists, and I did not speak out—because I was not a trade unionist.

> Then they came for the Jews, and I did not speak out—because I was not a Jew.

> Then they came for me—and there was no one left to speak for me.

As it relates to populating both the U.S. Senate and House of Representatives to install our elected rule makers and official referees:

- The Senate's "two per state" needs would be met by installing the top two, majority RCV finishers in the Senate races in their state.
- Congressional districts would get redistricted (yet again). Sorry, we can't get completely away from this cockroach-flavored issue. Districts would be redrawn to best balance the populations in each *and* maximize compactness (i.e., minimize the total distance of the district lines, in miles, across the state for the number of districts based on the census). The drawer of this "optimization" would be a math program, an algorithm, that would be used across *all* states. The algorithm would have to survive independent testing initially and be updated as needed over time. Each district's winner would be determined according to an RCV vote.

Campaign finance reform

The "who votes" and the "how they vote" questions may be clear—if only in our (my own?) dreams—but what about who runs and how they run? Specifically, how does the system avoid being overly influenced by money and connected people? Good questions that can be answered with just three words: *campaign finance reform*. It is in this realm that governance "levelling" might just have the greatest and most positive impact.

The U.S. Democratic and Republican parties are so powerful and well-funded, beholden to their contributors, that without campaign finance reform there's little hope of cleaning them up or making room for a third-party, centrist, candidate in today's extreme two-party polarization[30] to even be able to run, let alone be elected. Today, if third-party candidates are not uniquely wealthy or connected themselves, the minuscule possibility of being electable becomes, essentially, zero: hopeless. Let's get the distorting and corrupting impact of money out of elections with two major reforms:

- Let's make all campaign contributions exclusively limited by linking them to individual Social Security numbers (until we have safer personal identifiers). Contributions would be limited to 10% of that unique person's taxable income up to a $50,000 maximum. Corporations and unions (or LPs, LLCs, partnerships, and so on[31]) would no longer be able to make contributions in any way, shape, or form even though legally they are considered persons. Schumpeter's "creative destruction"[32] was based on a cycle of innovation—motivated by profits—which would see a birth and death of ideas; a kind of natural evolution of innovation. While corporations and unions (and other such entities) can die, their unnatural lives should not be extended by unnatural methods or political contributions.
- Political advertising on various media "channels" (television/Facebook/Twitter/etc.) would be available for free via a new broadcast requirement, imposed on a limited number of selected channels, that those channels offer an equal amount of time to four candidates for all elections. If there are more than four candidates or fewer than four candidates, the actual number would simply divide up the pre-allocated allotted time equally. Please note that too much choice (or information) has been shown to cause people to either not make any choice at all, or to regret their choices later. Simplification of the number of candidates (potential future leaders) is a worthwhile goal.

The role of all respective political parties would be to allocate funds to support their candidates' travel and other miscellaneous costs out of sequestered campaign

---

30 Pew Research Center, "Political polarization, 1994–2017" (Oct. 9, 2017), http://www.people-press. org/interactives/political-polarization-1994-2017/

31 In *Citizens United v. Federal Election Commission* (2010), the U.S. Supreme Court ruled that political spending is a form of free speech that is protected under the First Amendment. The controversial 5–4 decision effectively opened the door for corporations and unions to spend unlimited amounts of money to support their preferred political candidates, provided those entities were technically independent of the campaigns themselves. In my opinion, this ruling is a travesty that promotes crony capitalism and should be reversed ASAP.

32 Joseph Schumpeter, *Capitalism, Socialism, and Democracy* (1942).

contributions.[33] The use of public tax dollars for any political campaigning should become completely avoidable over time. Another key is that additional purchases of broadcast ads of any kind would be prohibited. Money would no longer have the impact that it has today.

Moreover, limitation to the predefined, predetermined media outlets would help to avoid the new—very real and disconcerting—technology abuses. First, you would know when and if you're seeing a fake targeted political ad rather than one that was "sanctioned." Second, the technology (which exists today) that can manipulate a person's likeness and voice so that we would hear and see them saying things they never actually said would be counteracted and neutralized. Genuine ads must be respected, protected, and trusted as such.

Governance can take on additional dimensions[34] beyond the who's and how's of voting

Consider the following ideas that counter other risks of crony capitalism, regulatory capture, or simply too much power/influence.

Term limits for politicians

Being of public service is a mindset, and a good one at that: but service should not be a paid career. The longer any individual holds an office, the more entrenched and focused that person's influence becomes. Let's enact a limit of no more than two terms of four years each for the U.S. president and state governors, and six years each for the members of both houses of Congress. The election cycles should be staggered to avoid too much turnover across too many offices in too short a period.

Also consider that with the limited channels of political advertising, we just might engender more voter interest and engagement. The nonstop, loud, blitz-style campaigns are more and more tuned out, if only by those outside of the party bankrolling them. Besides, the motivated "eyes wide shut or hands over ears" contributes to the polarization of our politics, and the total lack of attempts to even try to understand the other side's views. The public should never, ever feel election fatigue, and in a perfect world would be able to hear opposing ideas (like those in this chapter).

---

[33] Of course, the party "machines" would still work to determine who their most viable candidate(s) would be and assist in crafting the message to be delivered.

[34] One governance dimension that was in *Let's All Learn to Fish* was about defined benefit pension programs. The design of such programs is tremendously effective, but people and politics cause them to fail regardless of their sound design due to poor governance decisions.

Spending limits for sitting/incumbent politicians
While I acknowledge that this one is a bit "out in left field," what if clear "handouts" to any specific parts of the given electorate (known to all of us as bribes) were prohibited within 12 months of an election? Left field … or the right thing to do?

Lobbyist/lobbying influence limitations
Former government workers should not be allowed to become lobbyists following their government employment or to be employed by any company over which they had governmental responsibility or with which they dealt during their term(s) of office. My suggested "cooling-off" period is 10 years.

Let's also shine a very bright light on the corporate dollars spent to influence government workers. How about requiring corporate lobbying dollars to be clearly displayed on the "home" page of the corporation's or foundation's website, and require zero clicks or scrolling to view their spending? The information to be displayed could be: (1) the trailing 12- and 48-month dollars spent, (2) the equivalent dollar percentage as related to both the corporation's net income and total taxes paid for those time periods, and (3) the most recent 12-month year-over-year percentage change in spending. This "light" of disclosure is meant to aid transparency (and maybe act as a disinfectant, too), as it would make the information publicly available to everyone—including the corporation's employees, who may not even know what their employer has been contributing or to whom.

Transparency is only useful, though, when the information is understandable, which is not easily accomplished. The following is some evidence that supports strong regulation such as the proposed cooling-off period and disclosures:

> "It seems ever clearer that, when corporations open their wallets to politicians, the public loses."[35]

> "Congress does not have the resources to counter the growth of corporate lobbying. Between 1980 and 2006, the number of organizations in Washington with lobbying arms more than doubled, and lobbying expenditures between 1983 and 2013 ballooned from $200 million to $3.2 billion. A stunning 2015 study found that corporations now devote more resources to lobby Congress than Congress spends to fund itself. During the 2017 fight over the tax legislation, the watchdog group Public Citizen found that there were more than 6,200 registered tax lobbyists, versus 130 aides on the Senate Finance Committee and the Joint

---

[35] *The Economist*, "Bought and paid for" (Oct. 6, 2018), 70.

Committee on Taxation, a staggering ratio approaching 50-to-1 disfavoring the American people. In 2016 in the House, there were just 1,300 aides on all committees combined, a number that includes clerical and communications workers. Our expert policy staffs are dwarfed by the lobbying class."[36]

"Both intangibles and political factors account for a substantial part of the increase in profits, but since 2000 political factors are more important."[37]

With the progress made in artificial intelligence (AI) so far, let alone what's coming, lobbyists are less needed for the information they once provided than ever before. Given this reality, all that remains is influence and that's precisely what we need to stop. However, that does *not* mean that we shouldn't question the conclusions that come from AI-acquired information (more on that in chapter 4).

More governance reforms

Here are two more governance topics that, though not specifically about crony capitalism, are related and have risen to a level that is concerning to some.

Index fund voting

The proxy voting—corporate governance—for publicly traded companies owned by index funds has become a concern. Index funds basically buy and own shares of publicly traded companies in relation to their size (market capitalization: stock price x shares outstanding) in the market. Their stock selection method is purely mechanical and is based on other people's (not their own) estimates of the companies' valuation. Basically, the bigger the company, the more the index fund owns it.

The success and popularity of following this elegant approach has led to index funds owning a significant portion of all major U.S. companies. So, with only a few very dominant firms managing most of the index fund assets today, this means that the proxy voting (governance) process is controlled by ever fewer individuals. The question is whether we want such dramatic, concentrated voting in the hands of so few, especially given that they have little visibility or accountability. Furthermore, a couple of the dominant firms are also publicly traded businesses themselves, with their own proxy voting issues. I'm not saying that they're conflicted, but they certainly have conflicts.

Although some governance solutions have been floated to address this concern, none seem to solve the challenge simply or leave the elegant index fund structure

---

36 Bill Pascrell Jr., "Why is Congress so dumb?" *Washington Post* (Jan. 11, 2019).

37 James E. Bessen, *Accounting for Rising Corporate Profits: Intangibles or Regulatory Rents?* Boston University School of Law, Law and Economics Research Paper No. 16-18 (Nov. 9, 2016).

in place as it exists today. After all, index funds have been and are a very good thing for investors.[38] I suggest that all index fund proxy votes "mirror" the voting that is done by all non-index owners of the respective company's shares. With respect, to accomplish this, there would have to be a delay between individual company shareholder proxies and the final proxy tabulations; the delay would be necessary to add in the mirrored index fund votes following the tabulation of the non-index votes. Simple, less tainted, … good?

"Winner-take-all" businesses

Today, businesses have more global reach than ever before, may be based primarily on intellectual property (bits and bytes versus factories and manufacturing equipment), may have brands respected by billions, and may even produce nothing tangible (if they are mainly service-based operations). As such, some of today's businesses require very little money to grow compared with capital-intensive businesses like old-line manufacturing companies, which we still need.[39]

Such advantages for some firms have caused them to grow at rates never seen before, a result that has hurt competition and limits competitive threats in the future. These "winners" can also have real negative impacts on locale employment and wage opportunities. When few employers exist in a given area, the limited job availability and competition for jobs tends to limit wage gains—this is called *monopsony.* Venture capitalists—those who have the money and connections to invest in young or start-up businesses—have dubbed some of the competitive spaces in which winners operate as "kill zones" and avoid investing in young or start-up businesses in these zones.[40]

What is a winner, anyway? How about any company that is bigger than or equal to 15% of its sector out of the 11 broad economic sectors[41] that exist today in terms of its market capitalization? Based on a cursory review of companies that are perceived as winners today, 15% seems to be a potential threshold. For more competition, lower the 15% or use a lower threshold with the more numerous industry (versus sector) groups—but let's be careful of being too restrictive. By the way, does anyone even really know what's too restrictive? Upon a winner winning to that 15% level, and until

---

[38] *Thank you,* Jack Bogle (RIP 1-26-19), for your tireless work that brought the index fund to all investors.

[39] At least until 3D printing is much more commercially available than it is today, if/when that happens.

[40] What if the government stepped in to help fund some start-up businesses and future profits from those investments were used to fund other start-ups or help finance/enable childhood investments or lifelong learning?

[41] We could further narrow this to industry groups, but I hesitate to undertake such thin slicing. However, if we were to narrow, the threshold number would have to decrease.

and unless the winner falls back below a 10% slice of the sector, winners would "earn" (be saddled with) two additional regulatory restrictions:

- Stock buybacks[42] would be prohibited. Stock option rewards would become dilutive[43] and a bit more obvious. Financial engineering would be significantly reduced because borrowing via the issuance of bonds to buy back stock would end. Dividend payments or capital investments would have to increase, both of which could be beneficial for owners and possibly society too.
- Acquisitions by winners—of other young or start-up competitors—would not be allowed to exceed 0.1% of the winner's market capitalization in any rolling five-year period.

With these two restrictions, it could be foreseen that the growth of winners by other than organic means would be lessened, and competition would have more "space" to flourish. Maybe think of this as trimming the tree canopy to let more light get to the seedlings. It could also be foreseen that winners might spin out or sell off divisions to regain more flexibility and strategic control by shrinking voluntarily. In addition, the suggested limitations on lobbying would also certainly play a role in restricting winners' ability to dominate for too long. Never forget the benefits of Schumpeter's creative destruction.

---

[42] As an aside, stock buybacks have historically been more costly than accretive. In fact, "investment theorist Peter L. Bernstein proposed, half tongue-in-cheek, that "companies should have to pay out all their net income in dividends. If they needed money to expand, they would have to get investors to buy new shares" (quoted in Jason Zweig, "The hidden risk when you own stocks for the long run," *Wall Street Journal* (Mar. 15, 2019), https://www.wsj.com/articles/the-hidden-risk-when-you-own-stocks-for-the-long-run-11552662001). For those who correctly challenge the tax-favored nature of buybacks versus dividends, who is receiving the tax benefits if the biggest of all investors are tax-sheltered entities like pensions, 401(k)s, IRAs, and so on?

[43] Which we could hope would lessen their usage and the incentives motivating distorting short-term behaviors. Regardless, the move toward issuing restricted stock in lieu of options is very good and makes the options discussion moot.

Chapter 2: Work

"The pleasure at being the cause"

—Karl Gross

Let's begin with a little clarity. *Work* is something we do; a *job* is something we have. In most dictionaries, *work* is defined as either an activity or a task:

- An activity which involves mental or physical effort to achieve a purpose or result. *Synonyms:* labor, exertion, effort, slog, drudgery
- A task or tasks to be done; something a person must do. *Synonyms:* tasks, jobs, duties, assignments, projects, chores

Although the synonyms for the first definition describe work that few would think of as enjoyable or fun, more and more of today's work activities involve mental rather than physical efforts. It's not that mental efforts such as rote or routine work aren't slog-like, but that progress away from the physical drudgery that brings the risks of death, injury, and long-term health consequences is wonderful. Simple question: How many of our grandparents would see our current work as real work?[44] For those who in some manner sit at a desk, look at a screen, and poke at a keyboard, our grandparents might laugh at what we call work. Regardless, we should not forget that there are plenty of workers whose work still requires physical exertion or mind-numbing routine. In fact, in the United States, employers pay more than $1 billion every week to compensate workers for disabling workplace injuries and illnesses.[45]

---

[44] Until 1900, the work week was 60-plus hours and often dangerous; work fatalities were more than 300 per every 100,000 workers. President Harrison said that industrial work was as dangerous as being a farmer, which involved daily jeopardy of life and limb. Even after the 40-hour work week became standard, work fatalities didn't drop to below 100 : 100,000 until the 1950s.

[45] Liberty Mutual Research Institute for Safety (2014). *2014 Liberty Mutual Workplace Safety Index.* https://www.libertymutualgroup.com/about-liberty-mutual-site/news-site/Documents/2019%20 Workplace%20Safety%20Index.pdf

The second definition (the one emphasizing tasks) seems short-term oriented rather than what we may think of as full-time work or a vocation. Maybe this could be described as part-time work or side hustles versus 100% freelance or gig work? A couple of facts about gig work: the work is often related to a passion or skill, and the number of gig workers who do *only* gig work is smaller today (2019) than often believed,[46] as compared to many more side hustles. The passion connection is great and would seem to indicate that full gig work wouldn't be so bad. Aside from today's smaller-than-believed primary attachment to gigs, tomorrow may be very different if the fear of lost jobs in the future comes true or if attitudes toward work change a lot. Today's broad range[47] of primary versus side-hustle estimates looks like Figure 4. Meanwhile, forecasts about the future seem to imagine that 100% freelance/gig work will become a majority of the "jobs" in the U.S. economy within, if not by, the 2030 decade.

Figure 4. Independent employment

Four recent major studies found that a sizable portion of the 160 million US workers earn income by working freelance.

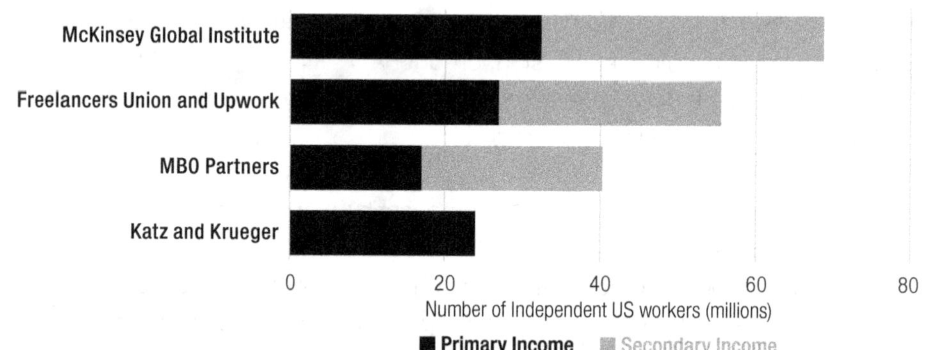

Sources: Lawrence F. Katz and Alan B. Krueger, The Rise and Nature of Alternative Work Arrangements in the United States *1995 2015 (RAND, 2016); MBO Partners,* State of Independence in America *(Herndon, VA: Freelancers Union, 2016); McKinsey Global Institute, "Independent Work: Choice, Necessity, and the Gig Economy" (2016).*

More to the point, work that is less than full time often does not provide "classic" employee benefits such as health insurance or a retirement plan. And, while retirement planning can be done relatively simply on one's own[48]—got financial literacy (?)—

---

[36] Josh Zumbrun, "How estimates of the gig economy went wrong," *Wall Street Journal* (Jan. 7, 2019), https://www.wsj.com/articles/how-estimates-of-the-gig-economy-went-wrong-11546857000?mod=hp_lead_pos5

[47] These ranges are broad in part because of the different definitions of what primary versus secondary income means. We are *not* clear on how many truly freelance or gig workers there are today.

individual health insurance is not obtained as easily or inexpensively. Although some may think they can just get another part-time job or gig to help increase income, these people should realize that negotiating several part-time schedules along with the respective, irregular demands from various bosses is *not* easy.

The dictionary's two definitions of *work* may be clear on "what" work is, but the why, the how, and the where (the *who* is you) are nowhere to be seen in the definitions. Interesting. Dated. Should all those details beyond "what" remain undefined? No. The lack of a broader definition is part of the (growing) problem.

Consider, if only for one, David Graeber's book *Bullshit Jobs*, which has somewhat taken the press by storm if you can judge by the reviews. According to Graeber, "we can probably conclude that at least half of all work being done in our society could be eliminated without making any real difference."[49] So, the $56,000 of annual per capita productivity (from the introduction) might be possible from only 1.5 hours per day? Really? Awesome!

Okay, now let's "slow our rolls" down and note that workers voluntarily contributed their stories to David's data and were solicited by him, via his blog on this topic—thus, his data were not really collected using any scientific method and were not confirmed by other researchers.[50] That said, I will not claim that David is directionally wrong, but rather that I am skeptical of the large size of his claim. So, why do these unhappy, dissatisfied, and disenfranchised workers stay in such jobs? Are these workers "stuck" due to prior financial decisions or life choices? Where's taking responsibility versus blaming?

While I do *not* wish to offend, I will take the risk of doing so to try to set the record straight. If prior less-than-good decisions have limited your choices today, that's not completely your current employer's fault. And, if you have choice, then stop playing the victim and leave those bad employers. Yes, I realize that you may have bills to pay and leaving is not so simple—I have experienced this personally. But leaving *can* be done.

Curiously, many of the people were in the banking and finance industries and allegedly proponents of the idea of bullshit jobs existing in their realm. Am I conflicted in my views (as I am in finance I could be considered a holder of one of David's bullshit

---

[48] Or with the help of quality behavioral "nudges."

[49] David Graeber, *Bullshit Jobs* (Simon & Schuster, 2018), p. 26.

[50] Robert Dur and Max van Lent, *Socially Useless Jobs* (Tinbergen Institute Discussion Paper 18-034/VII, Mar. 30, 2018).

jobs)? Nope. Maybe it's *not* all bullshit. The huge financial services industry has long been part of what seems to be eminently disruptable by technology (fintech), yet it has continued to grow and achieve ("earn" is questionable) handsome profits. Maybe the financial fiefdom is ironically being guarded by all those less than fully happy workers who won't quit? Hmm… curiouser and curiouser.

Might we have an incredible potential to increase everyone's well-being and we just can't recognize it or know how to achieve it? Is your glass half empty or half full?[51] Just imagine if we could shift from 1.5 hours on average (maybe not, David) to 3 hours on average (yes, let's start here) to 5 hours to 8-ish hours per day of work: imagine just how much that $56,000 could grow! Then again, how many hours in any eight-hour day are productive hours? Methinks that maybe we need eight to get five (when you mix in coffee/water/bathroom visits and web surfing aside from conversations that make colleagues into friends).

The nature of work today is changing, and the "classic" definitions may not be able to paint a complete enough picture. Let's take some time to better understand and to respect the why, the how, and the where of work today.

Why we work

Do we work to be the author of our own life's story, "to fund contentment,"[52] to have a purposeful life, for dignity, or to bolster our personal pride or self-esteem? Or do we work simply to pay our bills? (This could be the biggest reason across the population.)

Work that we personally value—"worthwhile" work in society, or Mr. Gross's pleasure of being the "cause"—leads to dignity, pride, and self-esteem; working just to pay our bills is a very different story. From the former perspective, work strengthens us mentally, just as exercise strengthens us physically. The latter perspective drains us, just as Graeber's "soul-sucking" (bullshit) jobs do. Please don't underestimate the importance of dignity, pride, and self-esteem, but do respect that "the biggest finding to emerge from the self-esteem movement was that praise did not predict self-esteem, accomplishment did. Telling someone that they are special is insufficient if they have not worked to earn it."[53] C'mon, even little kids know this! Doing the work is what's important. Why, what's your story? Answer this question: I work because …

---

[51] Sorry, it felt necessary to write this. For what it's worth, I have always questioned why no one asks about the size of that damn glass.

[52] Shout-out to a friend, Brian Portnoy, for this brilliant clarity.

[53] Daniel Crosby, *The Behavioral Investor* (Harriman House, 2018), p. 46.

a) I have a passion for doing X. In fact, I would do it for much less money (but shh …
don't tell my boss)
b) I want to be a part of something bigger than myself (are you under 40, a Millennial?)
c) I would like to fund my contentment (this response sounds cool, but what is your
contentment? And, what does that actually *mean*?)
d) I have bills to pay (ugh!)
e) I want to be wealthy and have nice things (and I don't need to apologize for that)
f) I have nothing else to do (do you see yourself as workaholic, are you over 70,
hobby-less?)
g) All of the above (wow, that's a whole lotta why)
h) None of the above (don't you work? If not, why not?)

In all seriousness, there are many good and varied reasons why different people work.
What if we take each of the potential answers to Abraham Maslow's hierarchy (see
Figure 5) to attempt more understanding?

Figure 5. Maslow's hierarchy of needs

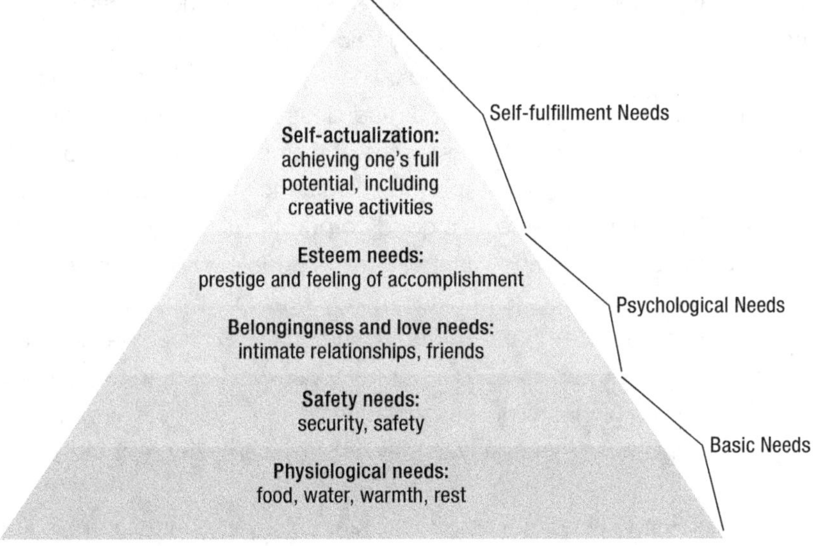

Interestingly, work has the potential to satisfy all three needs levels, but how much of
that potential is not being realized? A sad thought is that the three levels are not seen
as possible for as many individuals as we might otherwise hope. Then again, work does
not have to fulfill you; you can satisfy different Maslow needs separately. Regardless
(and this is stated with hope), work should not be a soul-sucking grind. Consider that

when you have an eight-hour workday and eight hours of sleep time, work represents half of your waking hours. That's a big chunk, if there aren't any needs beyond your basic needs being satisfied.

For the potential answers to the "I work because…" question, let's consider where they might show up on the hierarchy and whether our definitions of *work* do indeed need to shift.

The first three question responses: a) I have a passion for doing X; b) I want to be a part of something bigger than myself, and c) I would like to fund my contentment are ***all above basic needs***.

If "a," then do you consider your work to be a vocation, a calling? Do you relate to the quote "Find something you love to do, and you'll never have to work a day in your life"?[54]

If "b," then you might be curious to know about the 2017 survey from insurer MetLife.[55] MetLife found that 9 out of 10 people would choose to work for a company whose values are similar to theirs over a job that pays more. Furthermore, they were willing to take a pay cut to make sure those company values aligned with their own. In fact, the average pay cut employees were willing to take was 21%. Also, the findings were not limited to high-wage earners: People who made less than $50,000 a year also said they still were willing to part with at least some of their salaries in order to work for the right company. Three-quarters of respondents said they want a company that both supports them financially and acts as a good corporate citizen by demonstrating that it cares about the community and well-being of its people. Millennials were nearly twice as likely as Baby Boomers to put their money where their mouth is and take a pay cut to work at this type of company. (Author insertion for a little context: *generational cohorts matter!*) What's more, three-quarters of those who worked for a company with similar values reported higher levels of satisfaction with their jobs, were more loyal to their companies, and were more likely to stay with the company over the long term.

If "c," then do you know what makes you content? Funded contentment is about realizing the core things that make you happy, such as family, friends, or even your favorite meal, and perhaps recognizing that many of these happy things cost very

---

[54] Quote Investigator does not confirm the author; best is "an old-timer."

[55] MetLife's survey on *The Role of the Company* was conducted in July 2017 and was fielded by ORC International, a leading business intelligence firm. The survey comprised 1,006 interviews with part-time and full-time U.S. employees, ages 21 and over. The margin of error was plus or minus 3.5%.

little. Those who work for contentment—once basic needs are covered—often realize that work is satisfying only if the work is more of a vocation. Reflect on what makes you genuinely happy; I promise the time spent will *not* be soul-sucking.

The second two potential question responses: d) I have bills to pay; and e) I want to be wealthy and have nice things, are both challenged by basic needs or, in terms of e), what is called *lifestyle creep* (which expands basic needs and also includes esteem needs).

On July 31, 2018, Morgan Housel published a blog entry entitled "The Spectrum of Financial Dependence and Independence," and may have sliced Maslow's basic needs level into 16 strata through his specific focus on financial security and freedom. These two themes are important, because most of us began to work for income to satisfy a form of Maslow's basic needs. The following is Morgan's blog entry, reproduced (with his permission) from only an individual's perspective. Before you read on, ask yourself how your financial literacy plays into the levels, and allows you to escape the gravitational pull of Maslow's basic needs level. Please note my ***author insertions between some levels:***

Level 0: Complete financial dependence on the kindness of strangers who have no vested interest in your success. Panhandling when unable to work.

Level 1: Complete financial dependence on people who want you to succeed because they like you and their reputation is attached to your success. Children under age 15—supported by their parents and generally too young to work—fall into this category.

Level 2: Complete financial dependence on people with a vested interest in your financial outcome.

Levels 0–2 can create or enhance entitlement mentalities; that, in part, makes it difficult to rise above Maslow's basic needs level.

Level 3: Ability to partially support yourself by adding value for others while still somewhat reliant on external support. Young people who work but rely on their parents to support what they consider basic lifestyle necessities.

Level 4: Ability to fully support yourself by adding value for others, but value that is marginal and easy to replace. This is a common category for both people and businesses. It is grinding and tenuous. It smells like independence, but a boss or customer still owns your day and can dictate your future. Your future relies on their decisions.

Level 5: Enough savings to cover run-of-the-mill problems. You can endure hassles that every person or company should expect to experience on a regular basis, without getting wiped out.

Levels 3–5 begin to experience some financial freedom beyond satisfying basic needs.

Level 6: Enough savings to cover large, unforeseen problems. You still rely on your boss or your customers to get by month to month, but if a crisis struck, you'd probably be okay for a reasonable period of time.

Level 7: Retirement savings, education savings, and avoidance of consumer and auto debt. You still rely on bosses and customers, but you can foresee a time when your current savings will open-up a new level of independence for you and your family. This is the most realistic goal for most people.

Level 8: The ability to pick a job, or specific customers, that avoids the most egregious examples of bullshit and unnecessary hassle in your life. You still rely on bosses and customers, but have the freedom to say, "No, not you. I'll find someone else," when you get too frustrated.

It may be only after reaching Level 8, if you're up to it, that Maslow's self-fulfillment needs are addressable and possibly reachable.

Level 9: Becoming comfortable enough with your social status that you don't feel the need to flash your peacock feathers with expensive consumer goods whose only value is in signaling. The inability to do this is a hidden form of debt and dependence that exists, and it piles up on people who mistakenly think they're wealthy enough to be independent.

Level 10: The ability to say no to banks, whose debt you don't need, including mortgages. Debt can be cheap capital, but it keeps you beholden to others, owning a piece of your future decisions and cash-flow needs.

Level 11: Few realistic situations would cause you, your company, or your family to be pushed back below Level 5. You could support yourself for a year or more off your liquid savings. It's the first true stage of independence. You can now say "No" to almost anyone, with high odds of recovering from the repercussions.

Level 12: Interest and dividends cover more than half of your living expenses. Most of this is independence is owed to a slim lifestyle, rather than huge assets. You realize that lifestyle desires compound faster than almost any asset.

"Slim" lifestyles can help enable funded contentment. What really makes you happy? The answers for many—absent signaling—cost very little.

Level 13: Your assets and their reasonable return expectations will cover basic living expenses for longer than your life expectancy. Congrats. You are no longer reliant on bosses or clients. You can deal with them if you want, and you probably will. But only if you want, when you want, with who you want. Which feels good.

Are you retired, or simply continuing to do that which you love to do?

Level 14: Your assets cover above-basic living expenses with assets and their reasonable return expectations. You can define "above-basic" however you want—it varies by person. Remember what Chris Rock says: "If Bill Gates woke up with Oprah's money, he'd jump out the window."

Level 15: Independence lets you do and say what you please, unconcerned with other people disagreeing with you, since you don't rely on the support or opportunities they could offer.

How authentic you have always been, do you feel free to be who you really are, the "distilled" version? Would your friends remain your friends if so?

Level 16: Meaningful philanthropy is the only reasonable way your assets won't compound faster than you spend.

This is the only level at which a wealth tax could come into play … Sweet 16?

The last, final potential question response: f) I have nothing else to do … could be anywhere on Maslow's hierarchy based on the individual.

Where are you? If your reflection shows a workaholic, then hopefully it's because you love what you do rather than having few interests outside of your work. The reason for my wondering if you're over 70 is that this age cohort in the past often took responsibility to work to provide for or help raise their family rather than focusing on their own needs or interests. These individuals often know little else, and retirement for them can be uncomfortable because they have few (if any) hobbies. However, they can always pursue a variety of activities and adopt what resonates—that is what I hope for. But hope is not a strategy and this reality should be more known; let's get the word out.

If you don't work, why? Are you retired? If so, I hope you are at Housel's level 13 or higher. Are you incapable of work and in need of care from another, or capable and not working? If either, then Housel's levels 0 2 may have read to true to you. I shared Housel's 16 levels due to their wonderful clarity: not to define anyone's place, but rather to shine a light on aspects of financial independence and how it can so greatly affect our attitudes about work.

How we work

Let's first be clear: We are human beings, *not* human doings. Mike Rowe, the star of a television show called "Dirty Jobs," came to an interesting perspective after his crew and he experienced years of work that many of us might refer to as ranging from disgusting to dangerous. This is from his TED talk on his "Dirty Jobs" experience[56]:

> … some of the other things I got wrong, some of the other notions of work that I have just been assuming are sacrosanct and they're not. People with dirty jobs are happier than you think as a group. They're the happiest people I know, and I don't want to start whistling look for the union label and all that happy worker crap. I'm just telling you that these are balanced people who do unthinkable work … so I started to wonder what would happen if we challenged some of these sacred cows [like] follow your passion … Follow your passion, what could possibly be wrong with that; it's probably the worst advice I ever got. You know follow your dreams and go broke, right I mean that's all I heard growing up.

Wait a minute! Could the "pleasure at being the cause" trump most of the various why's? And, if that's true, then the how would be the key to satisfaction, dignity, pride, and self-esteem. Sadly, being the cause may not be enough given the present circumstances of many individuals.

> The economists of the early 20th century did not foresee that work might evolve from a means of material production to a means of identity production. They failed to anticipate that, for the poor and middle class, work would remain a

---

56 https://www.youtube.com/watch?v=IRVdiHu1VCc

necessity; but for the college-educated elite, it would morph into a kind of religion, promising identity, transcendence, and community. Call it workism. The modern labor force evolved to serve the needs of consumers and capitalists, not to satisfy tens of millions of people seeking transcendence at the office. It's hard to self-actualize on the job if you're a cashier—one of the most common occupations in the U.S.—and even the best white-collar roles have long periods of stasis, boredom, or busywork. This mismatch between expectations and reality is a recipe for severe disappointment, if not outright misery, and it might explain why rates of depression and anxiety in the U.S. are "substantially higher" than they were in the 1980s, according to a 2014 study.[57]

Thus, so-called "blue-collar" work (trades) can have some real advantages, as it can be largely nonroutine work which is less threatened by robots (see chapter 3) and generally does not require a college degree. Nevertheless, there are two genuine issues with today's workism: (1) ego-based identity production and (2) wrong-headed expectations.

Ego-based identity production is so interesting. First, are you (solely) what you do? I doubt those office or cashier workers would respond yes. Do the rest of us think we are solely what we do? If so, why? Is it because we receive psychological or self-fulfillment benefits from our work? In that case, workism may not be evil after all. If you do not receive any psychological or self-fulfillment benefits from your work and your work is your identity, then—please help me understand—*why do that*?

Wrong-headed expectations are everywhere. Are you familiar with the perspective that expectations are premeditated resentments? If your expectations are met, no biggie. If your expectations are not met, then come disappointment, frustration, and maybe even anger. Maybe we should stop having expectations? Absent such a superpower, just try to adopt a mindset of being of service, insight, or humor to your co-workers, customers, or clients. If appreciation follows from those co-workers, customers, or clients, you may be able to sidestep workism altogether. If no appreciation comes, then maybe you should go do your work elsewhere where people are treated like … people.

Workism seems connected to the topic of bullshit jobs. First, work does not have to satisfy needs on all three of Maslow's levels. Second, if you can lose the ego and the expectations, then you can probably say goodbye to most or all of the bullshit.

---

[57] Derek Thompson, "Workism is making Americans miserable," *The Atlantic* (Feb. 24, 2019), https://www.theatlantic.com/amp/article/583441/

By the way, there is generally and always plenty of work that could be done. At a minimum, consider that the American Society of Civil Engineers rates the U.S. infrastructure at a D-minus. There's plenty of work that has to be done[58] that could benefit the $56,000 per capita figure and improve the well-being of many. HELLO? This constitutes a huge potential fiscal stimulus, makes tremendous sense, and would certainly offer pleasures at being the cause; that's no bullshit!

Where we work

Where indeed, with today's technology? Let's first recognize and acknowledge that work is a thing we do, *not* a place we go.

With the advent of technology, does it really matter where many of us work, as long as the work gets done? No. Of course, some work is still location-sensitive, because we need to interact face-to-face with others or to access equipment. A "where" can exist, apart from those old-school (dated) bosses who require face time (no, not the app on your iPhone) as a surrogate for either their lack of trust or your lack of trustworthiness. Do you know ROWE™?[59] A Results-Only Work Environment™ is one where a leader provides clarity on what the worker needs to do, and then allows the worker to do it. Imagine how this could help guard against bullshit jobs. Trust is a key to ROWE's success, as are clear expectations from the managers and leaders. Too often, expectations are anything but clear (and risk breeding resentment), but do workers push for clarity? Often they don't. It takes two (sides) to ROWE. Do you recognize that ROWE, at its core, is about autonomy? And did you know that autonomy is a *big* intrinsic motivator that satisfies some of Maslow's psychological needs? It's also quite valued by knowledge workers (people who use their brain versus their brawn) and Millennials.

Let's better "enable" work

> *"I know of no safe depository of the ultimate powers of the society but the people themselves: and if we think them not enlightened enough to exercise their control with a wholesome discretion, the remedy is not to take it from them, but to inform their discretion by education."*
>
> —Thomas Jefferson

---

58 Jeff Desjardins, "The sad state of America's infrastructure in one infographic," *Visual Capitalist* (Mar. 23, 2017), http://www.visualcapitalist.com/state-americas-infrastructure-infographic/

59 ROWE™ was created by Jody Thompson and Cali Ressler. http://www.gorowe.com/

To better enable work, people first need to be properly prepared: educated or skilled-up and with entitlement-free attitudes about working. Is that too much to ask? No. It's clarity about how to take responsibility. Holding people accountable is exhausting, hurts relationships, and is prone to failure. Instead of trying to hold people accountable, try these three steps: propose an agreement, ask for understanding, and then get the agreement—on paper or in an email.

This is people agreeing to "take" responsibility. Of course, if it's truly an agreement, you can say "no"; clarity is needed to differentiate between what's an instruction and what's an agreement. What percentage of managers (leaders of people) ensure that "their" people are capable of doing the work and clear on the expectations for that work? Too few, you say. I agree wholeheartedly! To best enable work, of course we need to be clear what work is to be done, but to best prepare oneself to be sustainably able, think I will **"start early and never stop learning."**

The most important preparation begins in childhood—start early. So, the "I will" is a misnomer because it's really "others will" (on your behalf). When I start to think about this, I can't help but remember Dr. Seuss's book *Oh, The Places You'll Go!* (1990) and a few of his playful phrases:

Shoes, society, skills, and "space" to do what you can do … could this be any more about opportunity equality? Opportunity equality is not some wishful phrase, but rather an acknowledgment that we don't all share the same starting line. Regardless, wherever and whenever you start, an equal opportunity to race and *must* be available.

Got shoes? / Where you start matters!

This is the topic of opportunity equality: not everyone has shoes. Opportunity equality is not some wishful, utopian phrase, but instead an important acknowledgment that we don't all share the same starting line. Regardless, wherever (and whenever) you start, an equal opportunity to race and finish must be available.

Got resilience? / Can you, will you be allowed?

Failure happens. If you get back up from it, learn from it, and are better because of it, then can it really be called failure? Nope. We all need to be able to make our own mistakes[60] and not be overly protected, so that our resilience grows stronger. This emotional skill is advantageous, and you will see that shortly.

It's not just brains. While I would never, ever suggest that someone stop striving to be smarter, there are different types of intelligences. To what extent is your current work protected against today's workforce changes, and from the forecasts of disruption? Figure 6 shows some trends.

Figure 6. Workforce changes

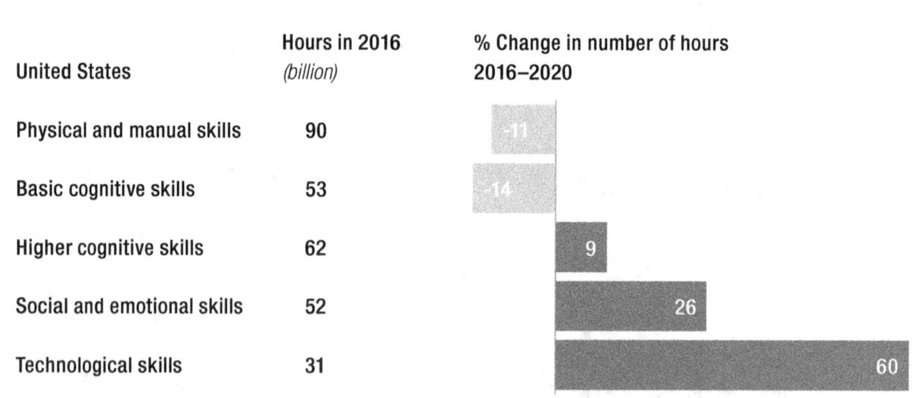

Source: McKinsey Global Institute, "Navigating a World of Disruption," briefing note prepared for the World Economic Forum (January 2019).

---

[60] Privately. This lack of privacy for our mistakes is among my biggest concerns/issues with social media.

We are starting to witness lost hours in some skill categories. Big brains (higher cognitive skills), though safe for now at +9%, are not nearly as safe as they otherwise could be with some additional skills. Genuine safety from disruption comes from having a big brain *plus* social and emotional, "soft"/noncognitive skills (such as communicating and working well with others), as well as being more resilient, and technological skills such as "directionally" big brains in a specific craft or advanced trade. Oh, the places you might go with more skills; "be dexterous and deft" indeed—thanks, Doc! For further evidence, see Figure 7.

Figure 7. The higher the levels of cognitive and noncognitive skills, the higher the earnings tend to be.

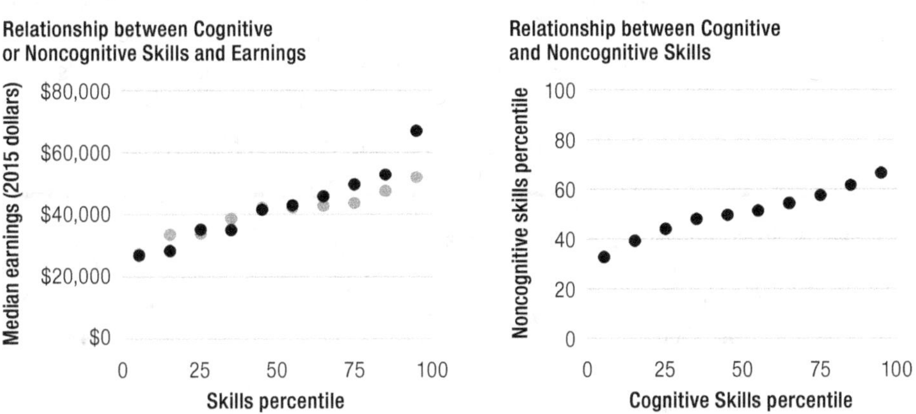

Source: The Hamilton Project Bookings. BLS n.d.a; author's calculations. Note: The sample for each figure is limited to men and women who reported earnings on the NLSY79 continuous income question, and who reported both an AFQT score and a noncognitive skill index score.

Start early (with help from others)

Recall, from the introduction, the intervention research that began at the age of 8 weeks and went until age 5: the societal result was a 13% per annum return for 30 years. Understand that one of the major components of that investment return was the ability to avoid—due to noncognitive skills—the courts, jail, and other such bad societal outcomes. There are many other studies[61] that demonstrate real noncognitive benefits from starting early. There are many positive externalities, too, according to Heckman:

---

[61] Another example—with participants ranging from age 3 to age 9 excluding kindergarten, and then followed to age 26—showed total economic benefits, per participant, to society estimated at $92,220 (about 10.8 times the cost) for preschool participants, $15,064 (about 4.0 times the cost) for school-age participants, and $42,520 (about 3.3 times the cost) for preschool- plus school-age intervention. Arthur Reynolds, Judy Temple, Barry White, Suh-Ruu Ou, and Dylan Robertson, "Age-26 cost-benefit analysis of the Child-Parent Center early education program," *Child Development* 82(1) (2011), https://www.ncbi.nlm.nih.gov/pmc/articles/PMC3817956/

[I]t's more than just stronger, richer, fuller lives for the children. It's also stronger, richer, fuller lives for the mothers of the children. Let me explain why. In America today, we have a lot of single-parent families. We have a lot of mothers who are working. What we've done is shown the benefits across two generations of the study of these enriched early childcare programs. Not only providing childcare for working mothers—allowing them to get more education—but primarily to get more work experience, higher earnings gains through participating in the workforce, but also getting high-quality childcare environments that turn out to be developmentally rich. It promotes social mobility within—and across—generations.[62]

Society has many reasons, not the least of which are strong financial results, to **start early**. So, let's get to work on early childhood interventions, if only for those who lack opportunty equality! Of course, this requires our leaders to include long-term strategic planning and not focus their spending solely on today (to get re-elected). After all, society will reap the rewards long after our current elected officials are out of office.

Figure 8 Employment Share Change (1850–2015)

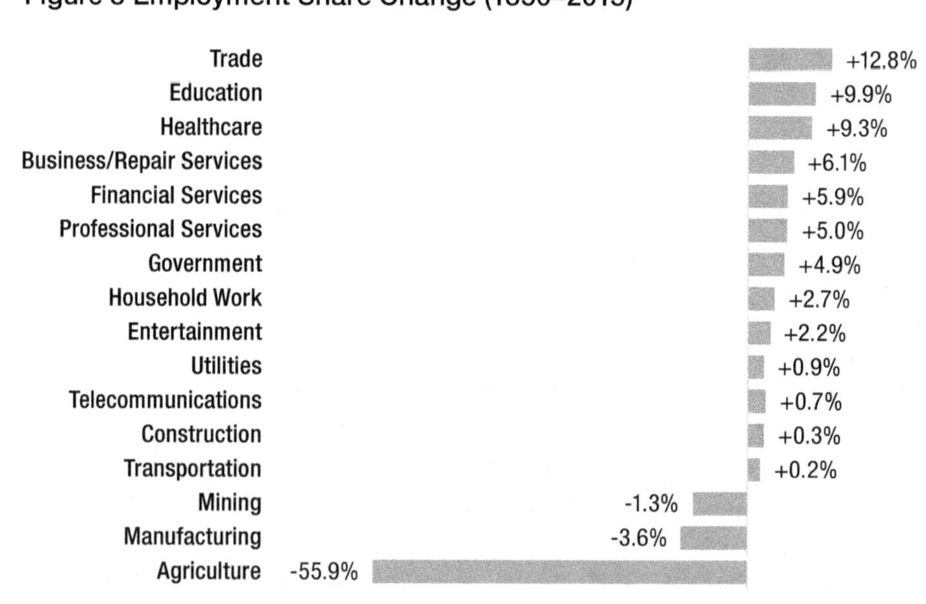

Source: IPUMS USA 2017; US Bureau of Labor Statistics; MsKinsey Global Institute Analysis

---

62 Eric Westervelt, "How investing in preschool beats the stock market, hands down," *nprEd* (Dec. 12, 2016), https://www.npr.org/sections/ed/2016/12/12/504867570/how-investing-in-preschool-beats-the-stock-market-hands-down (based on Heckman's research). See also https://heckman-equation.org/assets/2017/01/F_Heckman_CBAOnePager_120516.pdf

While we're talking about public schooling, a few thoughts on school days: Since we are no longer primarily farmers (see Figure 8), ENOUGH with basing the school calendar on the farming calendar!

- Begin later in the day, even if only for the teen years, to accommodate the hormonal and sleep-need changes experienced by teens during these key years.
- Attend school for more hours during the day to help enhance curricula, expand socialization, and provide parents more ability to deal with their work schedules.
- Expand school over more months during the year. This is less about more total school time—not that there's anything wrong with that—and more about shorter breaks.[63] Long summer breaks are not good: kids forget what they've learned and, again, parents can struggle with work schedules.

One study from the American South found that this "summer learning loss" could be as high as a quarter of the year's education. Poor children tend to be the worst affected, since rich ones typically live in homes full of books and are packed off to summer camp to learn robotics, Latin or the flute. A study from Baltimore found that variations in summer loss might possibly account for two-thirds of the achievement gap between rich and poor children by the age of 14 or 15. Long holidays definitely strain the budgets of poor families, since free school meals stop and extra childcare kicks in.[64]

Never stop learning

Now, *never stop learning*. Need an incentive? How about a longer life? (See Figure 9.)

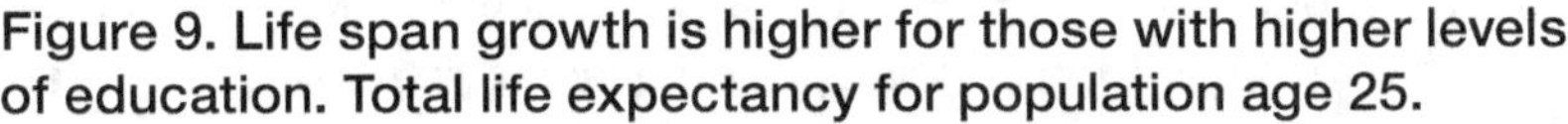

Figure 9. Life span growth is higher for those with higher levels of education. Total life expectancy for population age 25.

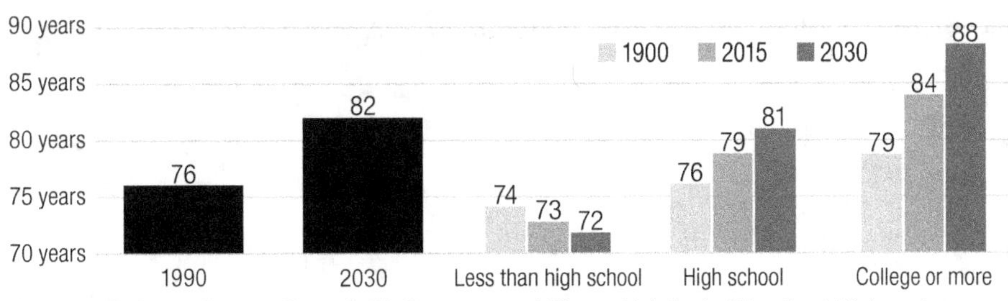

Source: U.S. Census Bureau, "Trends in Life Expectancy and Lifespan Variation by Educational Attainment: United States, 1990 2010," Isaac Sasson; Bain Macro Trends Group analysis, 2017.

---

[63] But let's keep enough break time to allow for other personal-growth activities such as camp, sports, music, cooking schools, and so on.

[64] *The Economist*, "School summer holidays should be shorter" (Aug. 15, 2018), https://www. economist.com/leaders/2018/08/11/school-summer-holidays-should-be-shorter

Higher education these days seems too much like a destination: "where" did you go to school, and "when" did you graduate are questions often asked by potential employers or people you meet (at least before you turn 40-ish). If our life expectancies are 80-some years, then how can we possibly arrive anywhere in our 20s or even 30s, and think we have arrived? C'mon! Let's create a plan for the steps needed to make lifelong learning a real thing and not just a goal.

Society could/should start by inventorying the knowledge and skills we have today. Then document the knowledge and skills society needs today *and* imagine what might be needed tomorrow to determine the today tomorrow gap. If imagining what work[65] will be needed is hard, don't worry: "making predictions is hard, especially about the future" (as Yogi Berra allegedly said). That's why the fear of job loss is so heightened even though history has shown that lost work has always been replaced many times over, although in different forms and requiring different skills. Today's fear might be a bit more justified based on the Dutch economist Jan Tinbergen's "race" between technology and the supply of education. According to Tinbergen, skill premiums and wage inequality increase when technology changes faster than the supply of skills (sounds a bit like today), and contracts when supply outpaces technology. Consider the past and future dimensions in "The Future of Work" graphic (Figure 10)[66] and ask yourself a couple of questions:

- Does the graphic's "Past" column represent simpler times, better times? Hint: perhaps only for those above a certain age or in leadership roles, and, more often than not, of a certain "pale" skin color.
- Does the graphic's "Future" column seem confusing, uncomfortable, and worrisome? Hint: again, only for those above a certain age or in leadership roles… that's called discomfort with change, especially when it involves you. Regardless, there is nothing in that forecast future that we can't do today, or that we can't upskill to handle.

---

[65] David Autor, "Why are there still so many jobs?" https://www.youtube.com/embed/LCxcnUrokJo?list=PLsRNoUx8w3rOyHeLmdk384sDpCq2GHwDw

[66] The Global Wellness Institute, *The Future of Wellness at Work* (Jan. 2016), https://globalwellness institute.org/industry-research/the-future-of-wellness-at-work/

Figure 10. The Future of Work

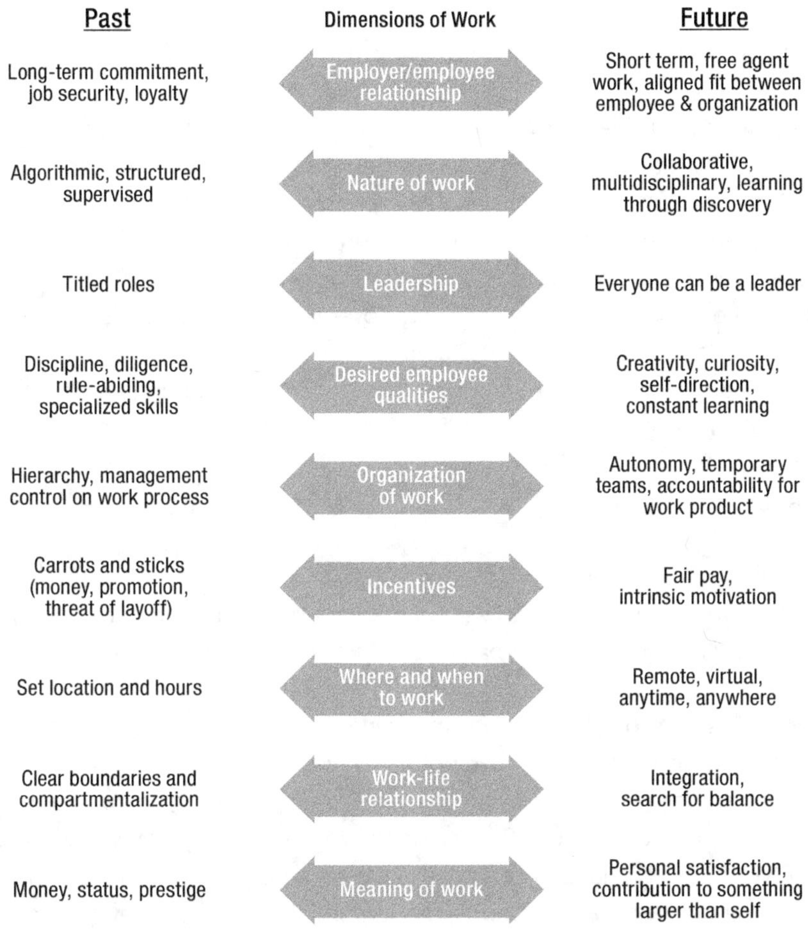

Did you know that the future is already here—to an extent—in part due to the wants of the Millennial and Z generations? By the way, when a generation becomes the majority in a population, they reshape that society in the way they want … for good or bad. The Millennials are forecast to be more than 70% of the workforce by 2025. That's another reason why my "cohorts voting" approach (suggested in chapter 1 on governance) can help. Maybe we shouldn't want any single cohort to reshape society. It's not about slowing down change as much as balancing majorities and minorities.

Try to understand what impediments exist to filling today's gaps, other than for those leader types who wish to hold onto the power they have. Sorry, the power is going to go, either the easy way or the hard way. Read the short, well-done article from the World Economic Forum for some ways to overcome such gaps.[67]

Let's begin to create/build for a better society:

- Create learning modules with some standardization (including the so-called soft skills) *to help broaden acceptance and universality for users and buyers.*
- Create a centralized database to track the efforts and accomplishments of those who complete these achievement/certification courses, for buyer work searches and reliable user verification purposes.
- Create partnerships with businesses, local governments, and schools (including those within the trades) *to help finance, promote, and support engagement with upskilling.*[68]
- Offer many access points, such as live classes, distance learning via technology (e.g., MOOCs), or in-house sessions in offices or manufacturing plants, *to bolster participation and make it easier.*
- Enable lifelong learning.

This harkens back to my prior book's safety nets and trampolines. Sometimes life happens. Will you bounce back, or will you need ongoing care and support? Most often (thankfully!), we can bounce back. Got a trampoline? Need one? Get one.

People who pursue lifelong learning are improving themselves and, in a sense, becoming less disruptable. However, if you have not yet achieved Housel's level 13, then you may need a trampoline of some kind. Do we need employers to share in or take responsibility for trampoline costs? Is that fair? Would we want them to do this when they eliminate a job? The idea of businesses having a purpose beyond just making a profit for shareholders is gaining popularity—and rightfully so—so why shouldn't they play a role in lifelong learning?

Do you remember when Bill Gates proposed taxing robots? What did you think of his idea? Regardless of what you thought about Gates's idea or even its appropriateness, such a proposal would have its challenges. However, employers who use automation to reduce employment could take responsibility for helping former employees move on

---

[67] Alan Tucker, "Lifelong learning helps people, governments, and business. Why don't we do more of it?" *World Economic Forum* (July 27, 2017), https://medium.com/world-economic-forum/lifelong-learning-helps-people-governments-and-business-why-dont-we-do-more-of-it-27144daa8c43

[68] Interestingly, it is reported that upskilling current workers is tougher than expected. Huh?! If you know your people, know their skills, and "understand" the roles/responsibilities/talents needed, then this should be doable. After all, it's cheaper than recruiting/hiring and better for current employees. A public private partnership may be just what's needed. In addition, partnerships like this will help with standardization for greater acceptance.

and bounce back. Although a former employee would receive unemployment benefits (a societal trampoline), such benefits are often not enough to live on and do not help the employee upskill or get a new job.[69]

What if the former employer paid one-third of its expected automation savings—from the change—into a lifelong learning fund (partnership, as mentioned earlier) within a given locality, and for a period such as 18 months? Employers could even be allowed to shorten the 18 months to 12 months through the offer and completion of a certified retraining program. Paths could be needs-based training programs that vary over time based on gaps and offered through any/all local or federal governments, private entities, or even employer co-operatives that resemble modern vocational schools. Lambda school[70] is one good example because of the way it's offered: as a distance program, with completion possible in less than a year, with skill(s) in current demand by potential employers and with a cost contingent on success (getting a quality job).

You may be thinking, *Why not just have the former employer pay the ex-employee a severance instead?* First, the local lifelong learning funding could have a multiplier effect, locally. Second, a direct payment could reduce former employees' motivation to pursue retraining/upskilling, so let's not take that risk. Third, the potential for a Universal Basic Income (UBI) will be reviewed in chapter 4 (patience, my precious…).

More importantly, why even wait for lost work with jobs that won't disappear but will require more and different skills? What if employers began to offer subsidized learning sabbaticals (such as every 5 or 10 years) for employees to upskill? Just imagine the employee loyalty this could engender, and the ever-better productivity that the employer could receive, aside from the cost savings from fewer employee departures (and new hire trainings).

If employers accept that they have a role to play, might governments offer any other trampolines beyond unemployment insurance, retraining/upskilling, or the potential for UBI? If UBI becomes a reality, then arguably a trampoline has been assembled. However, if UBI never happens, then the government might step in with the Brookings Institution's "wage insurance" idea. Holzer says, "Many workers who will be displaced over time but not retrained will likely face a future of lower wages than before or no work at all. For them, some form of 'wage insurance' makes sense. Such a program would compensate displaced workers for some part of their job loss—say, half—for a period of years. Thus, workers who formerly earned $30 an hour but only $20 now

---

[69] Which is both good and less-than-good (i.e., bad): good because trampolines should not become seductive, comfortable nets, but less than good because that introduces risk to the individual.

[70] https://lambdaschool.com/about/

would receive $5 from the government for a period, such as five years. They would therefore be incentivized to work and would also receive needed financial assistance at the same time."[71] Even if you don't agree with the specific time period and insurance amounts suggested in the Brookings blog, the idea has real merit: filling the gap between unemployment and underemployment. Of course, we would need to figure out how to pay for such a trampoline while balancing its costs against its benefits; perhaps among the range of potential UBI funding mechanisms (covered in chapter 4), one might work here. Then again, funding for wage insurance wouldn't be necessary if UBI happens.

Let's work (get) ahead

What if, broadly speaking, the most (wrongly) maligned generation—the Millennials—were a cause for optimism? First, they're a gigantic generation, and the growth in the number of workers plus growth in productivity is one way to measure economic growth;[72] the sheer size of this generation helps. Second, this generation has been alleged to be simultaneously lazy and purpose-driven. Huh? Might they simply be holding out for the purposeful job that so many graduation speeches seem to suggest? I suggest a look at the Japanese concept of *ikigai* (Figure 11).[73]

Figure 11. Ikigai

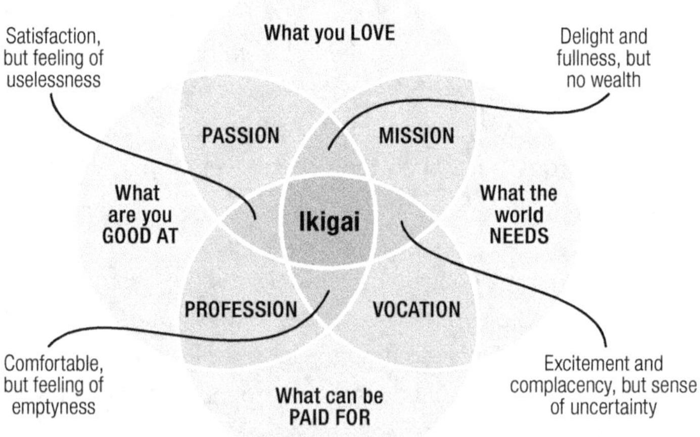

---

71 Harry J. Holzer, "The robots are coming. Let's help the middle class get ready," *Brookings Institution* blog (Dec. 13, 2018), https://www.brookings.edu/blog/up-front/2018/12/13/the-robots-are-coming-lets-help-the-middle-class-get-ready/

72 The clarity of this economic growth formula was a foundational piece of *Let's All Learn to Fish*.

73 The Japanese word translates roughly to "a reason for being, encompassing joy, a sense of purpose and meaning and a feeling of well-being." https://whatis.techtarget.com/definition/ikigai

Through the ikigai perspective, being purpose-/mission-driven can bring "delight and fullness, but no wealth." While I would never suggest a maniacal pursuit of wealth as the way to happiness, life does come with a price tag. Pursue purpose/mission PLUS. If you (strive to) embrace *ikigai*, your well-being is more likely to be achieved, and this requires some work.

Did you know that Millennials do more charitable giving than the X-ers and Boomers combined? Consider also their graduating college in or near the time of the "Great Recession," which meant some tough sledding when it came to getting work. Maybe those factoids offer some insight into their real or alleged socialist tendencies. Or could it be their sizable college debt overhang that makes them feel like they need to speak out against what feels like to them rentier (bad) behavior? Their "failures to launch" into independent life with some sense of financial security could spark an entitlement mentality in even the most responsible among us. How about practicing a little appreciation, now (is now good?).

Do you appreciate that the age cohort of 40 to 49 has been the most productive of all the age cohorts? The Millennial generation—the largest in U.S. history—is about to see their oldest turn 40. Hmm… the "everyone gets a trophy" generation we like to joke about could very well find their own capitalism and become productive based on their ethos. This could very well be something to cheer and not joke about. A little history is displayed in Figure 12.[74]

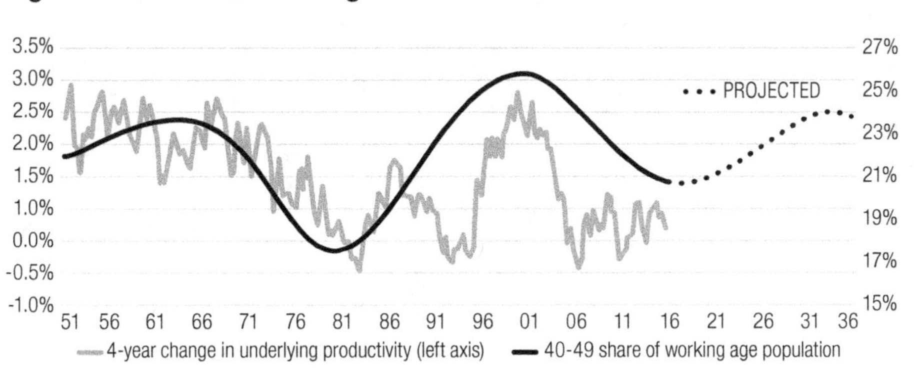

Figure 12. America's coming renaissance?

Source: United Nations; Federal Reserve Bank of San Francisco; Barron's calculations.

[74] *Retrospective estimates* are those made later by researching past data, rather than being estimated at the time. Graphic drawn by David L. Stanwick. Underlying data are from Stanley Lebergott, *Manpower in Economic Growth: The American Record since 1800* (McGraw-Hill, 1964), pp. 175 188. As seen in Matthew C. Klein's "The Economy" [column], *Barron's* (Feb. 8, 2019), https://www.barrons.com/articles/how-millennials-could-restore-american-prosperity-51549666748

The end of work (end of the chapter, don't get too excited)
While it may not be a popular view, there's no shortage of work that can be done and needs to be done. To paraphrase President Kennedy for the private employment world, maybe ask not what an employer can do for you, ask what you can do (as in work) to live your chosen life. Without able people working, productivity will fall and that hurts everyone, including society as a whole. So, PLEASE get to work.

"We do work, not jobs, and while some think that people owe us jobs they cannot owe us work."

—Mohammed Yunus, Nobel laureate

Chapter 3:
Us vs. Them?

"The future is already here. It's just

not evenly distributed yet."

—William Gibson

Who is the "them" versus Us? It's not the Millennials (*really?*) or immigrants (please stop being so entitled; we're all immigrants or children of immigrants). It's also not workers in other countries (globalization). Our current angst arises primarily (as in 80–85% primarily) from the wondrous productivity advancements[75] we have achieved over recent decades, through automation/technology. When you have a machine that can produce 10, 50, 250 times what any of us humans could produce without that machine in an hour, people's work capabilities need to evolve, because that work is going to be done by the machine.[76] Regardless, we do have to satisfy/satiate demand from well over 7 billion people on the planet these days. All productivity is good news for the seven-plus billion consumers (up more than five times in billions of 2014 dollars); the less-than-good news is how the machines and greater productivity abilities overall may continue to do more and more of today's work and thereby displace tens of millions of human workers (down more than 35% from the peak prior to 1980; see Figure 13). And what about tomorrow's work?

---

[75] A simple, wonderful example is the supercomputer that is your mobile phone, which is more powerful than all the computers used to land men on the moon, combined, 50 years ago this year.

[76] Machines will be replaced, too. I can imagine the tool-and-die machines talking amongst themselves and moaning about the coming 3-D printing capabilities.

Figure 13. Manufacturing Output vs. Employment

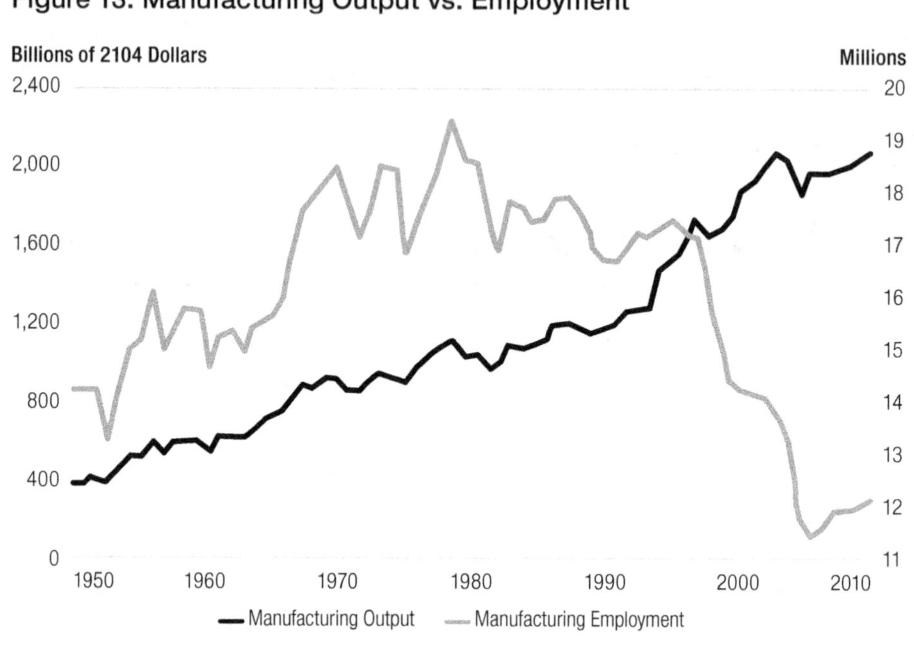

Source: Based on BEA and BLS data.

The "them" in the chapter title are the robots, anthropomorphized tech, versus the other automation/machines/artificial intelligence (AI).[77] However, who's complaining about low prices at their local superstore, or those online orders that arrive at your doorstep in a day, or safer work conditions? Pandering politicians may be trying to make us nostalgic for the past and "simpler" times ... Simpler maybe, but not better. There's nothing surprising about politician-speak regarding job losses. If politicians suggested that you take responsibility and upskill rather than blaming others for your challenges, they would need to upskill themselves (ironic?) because their probability of being re-elected would plummet. Figure 14 is an example of Jan Tinbergen's supposed race between people and automation advances and the forecast of losers.

---

[77] Could we please stop calling any machine that helps us do work a robot? Or do we just always anthropomorphize that which we see as an enemy? The laptop (and internet) that really helps me write this book is just my laptop—a tool—not an "assistant." I share this view with Laurence Siegel, as suggested in his book *Fewer, Richer, Greener*, http://www.fewerrichergreener.com (John Wiley, 2019 [forthcoming]).

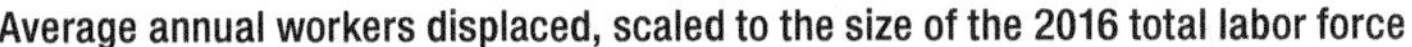

Figure 14. U.S. service sector automation could displace labor two to three times more rapidly than previous transformations

Average annual workers displaced, scaled to the size of the 2016 total labor force

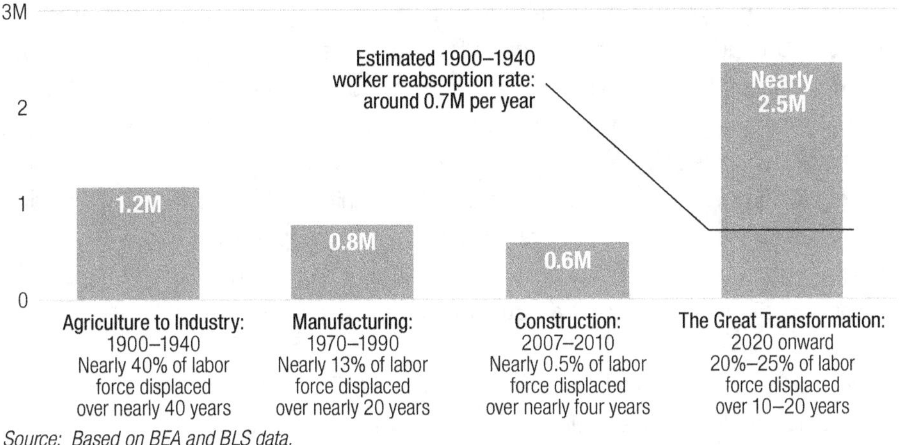

Source: Based on BEA and BLS data.

Well, Bain's forecast of a giant displacement coming[78] and looming reabsorption challenge seemingly could give a politician a heck of a platform. Ugh! How about we review the rules of forecasting? Rule #1—if you forecast, provide the event/forecast or the date but not both. Rule #2—if you forecast, update those forecasts regularly (as the best forecasters do, in all honesty). I have no quibbles with the quality of Bain's work, but let's be honest about forecasting; it's about the future, and the future is unknown. I have seen various forecasts of the percentage of people in developed economies who will lose their jobs to robots; they range from a low of 20% to a high of 60%. Why would you have any confidence in a range of forecasts that's so wide (apart from it being about an unknown future)? Nevertheless, people will get displaced, and there's no reason to expect that to stop in the future.[79] But with a larger global population and ever-better robots, the potential costs and implications of robot-driven displacements are bigger than before. I think Bain's forecast makes directional sense, but the number could be way off. Throughout history, lost jobs have been replaced by new ones and workers have been reabsorbed, although there can and have been lags. More rapid job losses due to ever-faster and ever-better robots will likely exacerbate lags. This ever-faster, ever-better is due to "adjacencies," as Shane Parrish put it:

---

[78] Just one other concern on the Millennials' radar that could spawn socialist tendencies.

[79] I remember when I graduated from university hearing that I would have six to seven different jobs over my lifetime (I'm on number three to five based on how you count), while graduates today are hearing six to seven different careers over their lifetime. Never stop learning … you're going need it.

The adjacent possible has been expanding ever since the first person picked up a stone and started shaping it into a tool. Just look at what written and oral forms of communication made possible—no longer did each generation have to learn everything from scratch. Suddenly we could build upon what had come before us. Some (annoying) people claim that there's nothing new left. There are no new ideas to be had, no new creations to invent, no new options to explore. In fact, the opposite is true. Innovation is a non-zero-sum game. A crowded market actually means more opportunities to create something new than a barren one. Technology is a feedback loop. The creation of something new begets the creation of something even newer and so on … As old limits and constraints melt away, our options explode. The exponential growth of technology is known as accelerating change. It's a common belief among experts that the rate of change is speeding up and society will change dramatically alongside it.[80]

However, lags do not always linger for long. Look at the historical unemployment rate (see Figure 15): it always seems to get pulled down, as if by gravity, to around 4%,[81] and keep in mind that's independent of the growth in the U.S. population, which was around 65 million people in 1890 and 325 million people in 2018. This is much more than reabsorption; it's real job growth from jobs that could hardly be imagined.

Figure 15. United States unemployment rate (1890–2018)

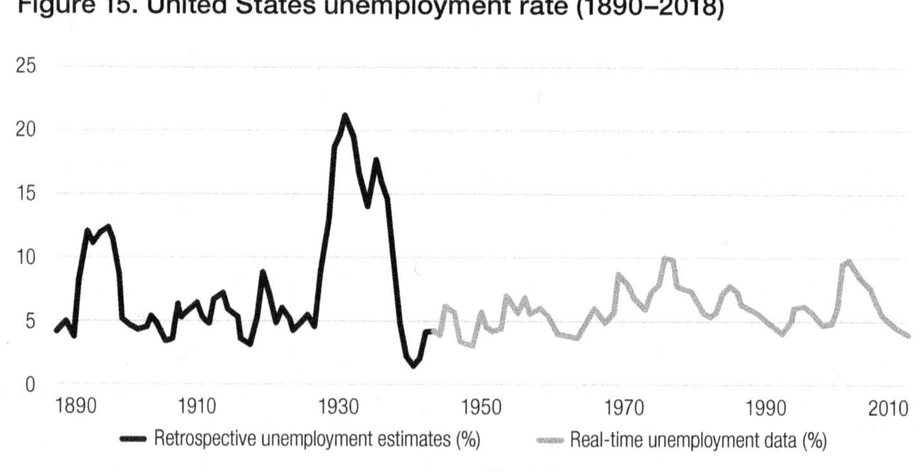

---

[80] "Gates' Law: How progress compounds and why it matters," Farnam Street blog, https://fs.blog/2019/05/gatess-law/. For an interesting, interactive tutorial related to adjacencies, check out Kevin Simler's "Going critical," *Melting Asphalt* (May 13, 2019), https://meltingasphalt.com/interactive/going-critical/

[81] *Retrospective estimates* are those made later by researching past data, rather than being estimated at the time. Drawn by David L. Stanwick. Underlying data are from Stanley Lebergott, *Manpower in Economic Growth: The American Record Since 1800* (New York: McGraw-Hill, 1964), pp. 175–188.

As much as we have always had lags, we always seem to return to about the same low level of unemployment. I propose that we only fear the lags (to new or better work), and not the robots. After all, who's going to design, build, maintain, and repair all those robots? Who's going to produce all the raw materials necessary to manufacture the robots, and ship those materials to the manufacturing facility? What about food for the workers who play roles in the manufacturing process, and their clothing, and their transportation, and their shelter? I could go on and on, but I think (hope) you get it.

We *can* upskill and retrain; better yet, let's embrace lifelong learning NOW and worry less about what some robot might (or might not) take from us sometime. There is always work to do, and that's without even trying to imagine what might have to be done in the future that's not being done today. Interestingly, the "what's next" work throughout history has tended toward better[82] and safer work. Nevertheless, let's recognize and appreciate (or at least try to) that the range of skills needed to work seems to be "barbelling": lower skills for services and higher skills for technical work. This creates employment polarization by shrinking the need for middling skills; jobs may not be lost, but those whose jobs aren't lost completely will likely see their work change and wages cut. A simple example is someone who loses a manufacturing job only to become a barista after a prolonged period of not finding similar manufacturing work. We are already seeing some of this today, and the unfortunate politics that can follow when an economy evolves but its (entitled) workers don't (think that they need to) evolve with it.

What if we peer ahead a couple of years or decades? Curiouser and curiouser it will get if fertility rates continue to remain low or drop further, immigration laws stiffen (or people stop wanting to immigrate), and the number of "eligible" future workers in developed countries like the United States drops precipitously without more retirement-age people working. Without a big enough, properly skilled workforce, reabsorption risks could disappear without "doing" anything, due to the genuine shortage of potential workers. Are you comforted by that information? We may *need* the robots to take jobs, according to Daron Acemoglu, a MIT professor, "Even if we have a huge acceleration in the adoption of robots, we are still talking about a few

---

[82] Greg Ip, "Workers: Fear not the robot apocalypse," *Wall Street Journal* (Sept. 5, 2017), https://www.wsj.com/articles/workers-fear-not-the-robot-apocalypse-1504631505

[83] Baristas, if not replaced by bean-processing robots, make for an easy example. However, don't forget that developed societies need help with their aging populations—and this care is real work. Robots will both taketh jobs and maybe giveth (via their unfragile construction) too. For example, today's exoskeletons (external "frames" that are worn either to help a person overcome an injury or to enhance the person's capacities through a system of motorized limbs that possess extra strength and endurance) help make people more mobile and stronger. Now imagine the further potential to lessen the need for caregiving if people were able to move better and do more on their own.

percentage points lower employment in the next several decades … . Research does not support a picture of the near future where machines will do all the work."[84]

Remember the "if you can't beat 'em, join 'em" phrase? Let's refashion that to be "if you can't avoid 'em, complement 'em." We're better when working with the robots, better together due to complementary skills. Consider the following example from tech entrepreneur Tom Gruber:

> [W]hen they combine the ability of the machine and the human together, accuracy went to 99.5 percent. Adding that AI to a partnership eliminated 85 percent of the errors that the human pathologist would have made working alone. That's a lot of cancer that would have otherwise gone untreated. Now, for the curious, it turns out that the human was better at rejecting false positives, and the machine was better at recognizing those hard-to-spot cases. But the lesson here isn't about which agent is better at this image-classification task … The lesson here is that by combining the abilities of the human and machine, it created a partnership that had superhuman performance. And that is humanistic AI.[85]

This type of superhuman joint capability has been seen across several domains, including chess competitions: Garry Kasparov—the former grandmaster who famously lost the "Man vs. Machine" match to IBM's Deep Blue in 1997—has said publicly that we, robots and people, are better together.[86] Beyond "safe" activities such as diagnosing disease or playing games, there are many potential benefits of having **ro**bot **pa**rtners (RoPa) when involved with dangerous activities or in less safe environments. Let's RoPa. The graphic from ZeroHedge in Figure 16 is a great example, showing that more oil and gas is being produced than ever and by far fewer humans; the dangerous work is being done by "them" ("who" are fewer in number too).

---

[84] Daron Acemoglu, "Will robots take our jobs?" *TNIT News*, Issue 17 (May 2017), p. 3.

[85] Tom Gruber, "How AI can enhance our memory, work and social lives," TED talk, https://www.ted. com/talks/tom_gruber_how_ai_can_enhance_our_memory_work_and_social_lives?utm_ source=newsletter_weekly_2017-08-12&utm_campaign=newsletter_weekly&utm_medium=e- mail&utm_content=bottom_left_image

[86] Garry Kasparov, "May 11: One big loss for a man, one giant win for mankind," *Medium.com* (May 11, 2017), https://medium.com/@GarryKasparov/may-11-one-big-loss-for-a-man-one-giant-win- for-mankind-46bb42b8752f

Figure 16. Oil and gas industry employees vs. rig count

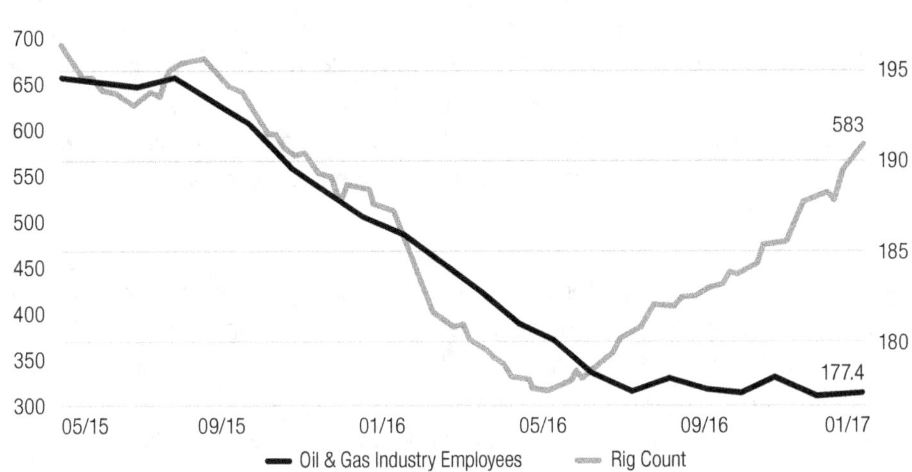

Source: ZeroHedge (https://www.zerohedge.com/news/2017-02-03/rig-count-surges-again-16-month-highs-wheres-oil-industry-jobs).

Ironically, as we move toward renewable energy, those "them" will lose, too, to other "thems" (built for another purpose).

The "Us" in this story will remain in demand, at least for a while, and for some commonsense reasons. First, businesses that invest in robot workers have significant up-front, "sunk" costs for those robots; such costs work best when spread across high(er) sales volumes. Small sales volumes do not easily support the up-front costs or even justify robot workers. This is an obvious truth for small(er) businesses, and these businesses have long been the real drivers behind job creation in an economy.[87] An interesting question, maybe, should be asked about employment beyond small employers. In a world that's about work, your talent, your work/life balance, your purpose, and so forth, it would seem that you, the worker, would be able to find the great "fit" among many small employers (if you don't become one yourself).

Why wouldn't most employers of the future tap into the abundant, worldwide pool of talent and skills? They could outsource specific needs, crowdsource all or part of certain tasks to be completed, and remain small, if only for longer? Today, companies hold crowdsourcing contests with big dollar prizes to solve deep research questions

---

[87] But will this continue to be true, regarding size? Small businesses are economic engines and employers, and deserve supportive polices to help defend themselves, if only against monopsony risks.

and other challenges they have.[88] What if that approach went viral, reaching a greater variety and types of work that employers have historically hired employees to do? This would be a gig economy on steroids, and not just for those considered freelancers. Of course, this could only happen with people who take responsibility, obtain clear agreements on what work is to be done, and get compensated fairly for the work being done; there would also have to be a shift in benefit policies (mainly health insurance) as well as improved work/worker regulations. Okay, enough pontificating about a possible future.

The second commonsense reason is that not all jobs entail only routine-type work. The third reason is that not all jobs are solely made up of single-domain responsibilities, as in "do x to get y." Deep Blue is "brilliant" at chess but couldn't answer a question about what ingredients are necessary to make cookies or drive a car. Deep Blue was programmed by humans to play chess but not do anything else. Think of robots simply as extensions of humans.

Today, robots are wonderful with repetitive or single-domain tasks. Think "find this" or "do that." The capabilities of robots today offer "Us" freedom from risky, mind-numbing, and redundant work. Good! Hmm… today's robots seem a bit like the classic hedgehog that knows a few things deeply or does a few things very well versus the fox that can operate across or in many different domains. Robots do not discriminate in the work they do (they are programmed, or machine-"learn" on their own to do X) or call in sick, but currently their capabilities are severely limited to single domains. Multidomain, cross-domain, or what we might call "in the wild" robot skills—so-called artificial general intelligence (AGI)—is in the future, if we ever actually achieve that level of progress. AGI has real skeptics. Those current limitations allow Us to be more "human" in our work, work that is arguably more about creativity, includes other people, or crosses multiple domains—i.e., better work. However, better work is not better for everyone today based on their individual skills.

If robots are hedgehog-like, then many people will be better off being more fox-like. This observation takes us back to chapter 2's discussion of how best to enable work and lifelong learning. Do you recognize that our educational systems were built for foxes (good)? However, education beyond high school or with many vocational schools, the designs are for hedgehogs. Although hedgehogs will absolutely be needed in society, let's improve how we educate and train people, to bolster our human, fox-like

---

[88] Now imagine the world's subject matter experts (SMEs) and how they could be crowdsourced for all sorts of day-to-day thinking tasks and paid per "gig."

advantages. Regardless, don't completely write off robots as being incapable of at least mimicking creativity through brute-force repetition (trial and error) and randomization,[89] or evoking emotionality (as seen in how people respond to small, furry animal "comfort" robots). Robots can and will simulate behaviors that in many ways we may find human-like, even though they are not.

Fear the lag? Yes. But what if the lag is less scary? For all the fearmongering and handwringing about a robot job-stealing apocalypse, there are growing reasons why the speed of job replacements may not maintain the same level of job destructiveness as it has or wreak as much havoc as people think. First, history has shown varying lag periods. Second, there are two real and important growing, governing hurdles for robots to leap: data and fairness.

Data, data everywhere, but (maybe) not a nutritious "byte" to eat

For this section, I shift from robots to "AI" to help with clarity. AI stands for artificial intelligence. The artificial is from either programming (a formulaic approach) or machine learning/statistical inference drawn from access to tremendous amounts of data. "Big data" can be helpful or harmful.90 When we reference AI today, it's most often the machine learning (ML) approach. ML depends on just two things: computing speed (to do the statistical work) and data. Today's high computing speed is enough, but it's getting even faster and poised to make a gargantuan leap forward when quantum computing becomes commercially available (maybe by 2030). Today's data, though abundant, is an ever-present challenge. Why? A piece of data is an "artifact" from a point in time, public or private, in a sea of potential context that may be trending or may simply be specific to that point in time. Imagine a painting and then imagine it as millions of equivalent color pixels; could you see the painting from the pixels, if they were randomized in space? Consider the following five key data questions:

1. *Is enough data saved, accessible, and usable?* First, "enough" is relative to the need; one may question whether we can even answer how much is enough. When businesses launch what they consider AI projects, they can learn that "10% of the work is AI, ninety percent of the work is actually data extraction, cleansing,

---

89 Emerging Technology from the arXiv, "Deep-learning machine listens to Bach, then writes its own music in the same style," *MIT Technology Review* (Dec. 14, 2016), https://www.technology review.com/s/603137/deep-learning-machine-listens-to-bach-then-writes-its-own-music-in-the-same-style/?utm_medium=tr_social&utm_source=linkedin&utm_campaign=site_visitor. unpaid.engagement

90 All this inferring means that even without your personal data, your friends' and cohorts' data help enable the understanding of you. For a short, sobering read on this, see Martin Tisné, "Data isn't the new oil, it's the new CO2," *Luminate* blog (July 24, 2019), https://luminategroup.com/posts/ blog/data-isnt-the-new-oil-its-the-new-co2

normalizing, wrangling."[91] AI offers the ability to "see" the painting that exists by viewing thousands of pixels. Do businesses know and own "their" pixel data to "see" their painting? What happens when some portion of their pixels might be considered external to their business, such as client demographics? Maybe there would be no painting available to see. Data is not simple, and its usability or privacy issues will continue to be problematic. To paraphrase a famous campaign strategy meme, "It's the efficacy of the data, stupid!" There's also a business ethics aspect to using data, even when it's quasi-internal, such as with data related to a business's own employees. The ethics issue is a topic unto itself, so there's more on this later in this chapter.

2. *Who owns or controls the data used?* This question connects with accessibility. Whose data is it, and who can claim ownership or permission to use it? Think Amazon, Facebook, Google, and so on (and these are only U.S.-based businesses, let alone China-based "state-overlords"). Put simply, data is not often, if ever, open-sourced; yet it is seemingly owned and leveraged for individual corporate profit reasons. This limits the value of much of the data to the primary aggregators/owners, a situation that tends to benefit winner-take-all types of businesses and limits AI's potential for public use and benefit.[92]

We (the people) should have the final say on the usage of our data. If it's available for open-source sharing, resulting in benefits to the public, then we should expect an amount of privacy. If it's used for private gain, then shouldn't we expect payment? Can you hear the chant rising "give me privacy or give me payment" with respect to our personal data so that we are not the product?[93] Following this theme, what if private companies paid people—after receiving permission to use their data—a flat rate "per piece of data or period of time," or if the businesses paid "data taxes" … like 5%, for example, of their top-line sales (to help prevent any financial gaming)?[94] However, even if these businesses paid a data tax, they would still owe a level of privacy to the individuals whose data they leverage.

---

[91] Brian Bergstein, "This is why AI has yet to reshape most businesses," *MIT Technology Review* (Feb. 13, 2019), https://www.technologyreview.com/s/612897/this-is-why-ai-has-yet-to-reshape-most-businesses/

[92] Geoff Mulgan and Vincent Straub, "The new ecosystem of trust," *Nesta* blog (Feb. 21, 2019), https://www.nesta.org.uk/blog/new-ecosystem-trust/. This is very good, thorough coverage of data for public good and privacy.

[93] In 1973, the artists Richard Serra and Carlota Fay Schoolman broadcast a short video titled "Television Delivers People." This was a precursor to the more famous "If you aren't paying for it, you're not the customer; you're the product being sold" by Andrew Lewis in 2010.

[94] This could make for some interesting, dedicated funding for a social benefit such as UBI; see chapter 4.

3. *To what extent is today's data predictive?* Another term for predictive is correlated—when correlation indicates causation. However, correlation of data might just be coincidental or weakly influenced with no real causal predictiveness. Sorry, but data is only useful to the extent that it is predictive and that it repeats. There are some, such as Judea Pearl (father of Bayesian networks, an extension of age-old probabilistic reasoning), who wish that AI systems built in causation to better understand the real world (but as of today they don't, and maybe not as of any tomorrow either).

   As an example of the intrinsic limitations of data-centric systems that are not guided by explicit models of reality, consider a risk-estimation model for those hospitalized with pneumonia. From the data, the model learned that asthmatics are less likely to die from pneumonia. Counterintuitive? Indeed. The researchers traced the strange result back to an existing policy underlying the observed data: asthmatics with pneumonia were immediately admitted directly to the intensive care unit, therefore receiving more aggressive treatment earlier, and thus were less likely to die than patients not given the same attention.[95]

4. *To what extent will data collected continue to be meaningful in the future?* This is a tough one; the future is unknown. Today's data would certainly be meaningful for some time before its relevancy drops, but we cannot know when that drop will occur. One way in which we might know "when" would be if there is a market in the data, when and if "give me payment" happens. When and if data universes change demonstrably (as in the amount or types of content), such changes raise questions and highlight a real limitation of any prior versus subsequent data. Tastes change, and whose tastes are we even talking about? Complexity and unpredictable changes seem more like the norm than the exception today. For example, global warming is[96] playing a significant role in forest fires and floods, but we know very, very little about where and when they will occur.

5. *To what extent are data flows consistent?* Like the meaningfulness of data in the future, how will similar—if not the same—data streams flow over time? GDPR! Those initials do *not* stand for the God Damned Privacy Regulation (should they?), but rather the General Data Protection Regulation[97] instituted in Europe. Similar

---

95 Alexander Lavin, "AI needs more why," *Forbes* (May 6, 2019), https://www.forbes.com/sites/alexanderlavin/2019/05/06/ai-needs-more-why/#162690a156d1

96 I do not know if global warming *is* playing a significant role, but Pascal's wager should instruct us to accept that it is; the downside costs and impacts are so significant that it's cheaper (a better bet) to behave as if global warming is in fact playing that role and we should act *now*.

97 Matt Burgess, "What is GDPR? The summary guide to GDPR compliance in the UK," Wired (Jan. 21, 2019), https://www.wired.co.uk/article/what-is-gdpr-uk-eu-legislation-compliance-summary-fines-2018

types of regulations are coming to all nonauthoritarian countries and businesses wishing to do business in nonauthoritarian countries (at some point, we can hope). Well, when the flows—amount or type of data—change, so too might AI's conclusions.[98] Tastes may or may not remain the same, but what you know about them would change. As privacy demands grow louder, data flows are going to be affected. How? I don't know, other than they will be affected.

The bottom line is that without good, deep, consistent data flows, machine learning (ML) techniques would be hamstrung.[99] AI interrupted! Since AI can be so positive for societal advancement, maybe let's *not* be encouraged by potential interruptions and instead pursue open-source sharing, privacy protections, data taxes, an ethical framework (next section), and ensuring that capable people remain a part of the "system" as inefficient yet robust pieces of the equation.[100] On a more individual note, because AI does its great work by "normalizing and wrangling" data, there are also real opportunities to leverage AI as an insightful coach that nudges *you* toward leveraging your strengths, or drives businesses to better understand their own competitive edges and their client/customer feedback—more RoPa.

Fairness

First and foremost, *fairness* cannot be universally defined; it's in the eye of the beholder. For example, what's fairer: a level dollar amount of taxes paid by people or a level percentage of people's income taxed? Point made? Okay. Let's respect that most data sets obtained or used, the programming done by coders, and the learning done by ML, could be biased in some manner. Results could be deemed unfair. Most data and programming contain biases from the data or the coder (both intentionally and unintentionally) which then become "hard coded" as part of results by the normalizing and wrangling of AI.

You do know (right?) that automation is used in credit decisions, to set insurance rates, in judging job applications, for college acceptances, and in prison sentencing, to name a few. Furthermore, ML will reach conclusions—but why? If we don't understand how the dots (data) were connected, because the decision-making process relies strictly on statistical correlations, we would lack understanding of and intuition about the result. This leads to either requiring us to trust and follow the AI pretty much unquestioningly, or to lose its potential value. Let's subject all results to a diverse panel

---

[98] A nod to John Maynard Keynes's (attributed) response when accused of changing his mind.

[99] However, in any given period of time, AI will undoubtedly appear brilliant ... until it won't.

[100] Thank you, Margaret Heffernan, for this elegant perspective on people as inefficient but helping increase the robustness. As Pablo Picasso said, "Computers are useless. They can only give you answers."

of (human) individuals whose job it is to observe and document patterns in results to help diagnose levels of bias or infer causation.[101] Although some biased results may be obvious, locating where the bias came from is important. As to how the bias was created, it may not be possible to determine this with ML, due to its billions of "learning steps" which could lead to its nonobvious conclusion(s). Regardless, if AI is to benefit society—and it certainly can—it has to be trustworthy.

Should we consider maintaining a human being in the decision loop prior to any "automated" decision-making, as a potential brake? Think of driver-assisted robo-cars. The driver (the brake) would be a kind of "free won't" to the AI's automated "free will." Second-guessing all decisions would be impractical, so no on the "all" case. However, for decisions that have significance or are not (easily) reversible/rectifiable in the case of an error, I say yes. But keep in mind that there is a lag in human reaction time to any stimulus. Again, think of a driver-assisted robo-car: the driver who needs to take back control in a split second will almost certainly do so too late, even if the resumption of control does not require being distracted from whatever else the driver might be doing. In other circumstances, such as fewer real-time response demands, free won't "interventions" would be valuable. We would need to train those who would be responsible for stepping on the free-won't brake; moral philosophy skills may be beneficial. The types of free won't decisions will likely be ethically challenging. The classic trolley experiment[102] from the 1960s highlights such an ethical challenge. You are given the choice to spare five lives in exchange for one (to whom you have no connection or contact with). Ninety percent of people make the choice to end the one life versus the five. However, when the choice is reframed as killing one person (as with a shove or push to their death) in order to spare the five lives, only 10% of people make that choice. It seems that anonymity has some absolution properties.[103] You do realize that yesterday's trolleys might just be tomorrow's robo-cars, right? Will the robo-car spare people on the side of the road or its passengers? And what's the right thing to do? By the way, the moment the robo-car makes either choice, the choice could be the end of robo-cars[104] ... if AI is not deemed trustworthy by society.

So, how do we find an answer? Perhaps we should look to 1971, the year in which philosopher John Rawls proposed the "veil of ignorance" in his book *A Theory of*

---

[101] The "diverse" component (e.g., cognitive, age, gender, ethnicity, etc.) is important to help minimize the biases of any such panel and help make sense of counterintuitive AI conclusions.

[102] Eleanor Nelson, "Would you sacrifice one person to save five?" TED talk (Jan. 21, 2017), https://www.youtube.com/watch?v=yg16u_bzjPE) highlights the base issue well (many dimensions and variations are possible). http://moralmachine.mit.edu/ lets you play along as well as compare yourself.

[103] This is part of why social media postings can be so LOUD and accusatory; how many of us would be so BOLD in person?

[104] Why driver-assist is fine while driverless robo-cars (self-driving vehicles) are in the future.

Justice. His "veil" was a thought experiment in which nobody knew who they were, who they might become, where they were (what they possessed, how old they were, etc.), and they were then asked how they would wish society's laws and norms to be in order to protect their status once the veil was dropped. In the trolley experiment, you could have been among the five lives being spared, the one life condemned (or pushed), or the one deciding in the experiment. What set of laws or norms would/could "work" for each of the seven people (everyone), once the veil was dropped and the roles were randomly determined? Well, given that someone or some will die, it would seem everyone would need to be aligned on the decision rule (process) versus the result. Okay. The basis of how the decision gets made is the key: for example, should five simply be prioritized over one and that's it? Or, when and if should other data (e.g., age, education, work, family, family financial situation, etc.) be factored in? If other data are used, then how should that other data be prioritized? Consider the following data set:

- The "one" by the track is a 40-year old family man with two young children.
- The "five" are all retired; two of them have prison records, three of them have grandkids, and the average age across the five is 71.
- The "one" pulling the track lever or pushing the "other one" is a single 49-year old.

Should any or all of that data count? If so, to what extent? Note that my data set is heavily biased; data is not always so clear-cut. What about pursuing more data that could potentially alter your thought on the ethical choice? Perhaps a diverse group[105] of moral philosophers might be able to draft decision criteria that would undergo a period of public comment before any decision criteria could be adopted.

AI designers need to take responsibility for their "captive" systems before those systems are released into the wild; let's require testing and auditing before any release. In addition to decision criteria, the other critical item is forgiveness. "Forgiveness" in this sense means that a form of nonreligious absolution and zero legal exposure/liability would apply to all decisions that satisfy the adopted decision criteria. This would be critical to success. Clarity and transparency on the decision criteria plus unequivocal forgiveness is the only way forward.

---

[105] Who are diverse across age, gender, ethnicity, thinking styles … and are citizens who are qualified to vote?

Is the AI glass half-empty or half-full for us?

Half-empty—If thought of as all-knowing. Daniel Dennett writes:

> AI in its current manifestations is parasitic on human intelligence. It quite indis-
> criminately gorges on whatever has been produced by human creators and
> extracts the patterns to be found there—including some of our most pernicious
> habits. These machines do not (yet) have the goals or strategies
> or capacities for self-criticism and innovation to permit them to transcend their
> databases by reflectively thinking about their own thinking and their
> own goals.
>
> …
>
> THE GAP BETWEEN today's systems and the science-fictional systems dominat-
> ing the popular imagination is still huge, though many folks, both
> lay and expert, manage to underestimate it.[106]

Half-full—If thought of as a great tool (that's verifiably safe). David Rotman, the editor of *MIT Technology Review*, writes that AI's greatest economic impact could come from its potential as a new "method of invention" that ultimately reshapes "the nature of the innovation process and the organization of R&D." Iain Cockburn, a BU economist and coauthor of the paper, says: "New methods of invention with wide applications don't come by very often, and if our guess is right, AI could dramatically change the cost of doing R&D in many different fields." Much of innovation involves making predictions based on data. In such tasks, Cockburn adds, "machine learning could be much faster and cheaper by orders of magnitude." In other words, AI's chief legacy might not be driverless cars or image search or even Alexa's ability to take orders, but rather its ability to come up with new ideas to fuel innovation itself.[107]

Another distinctly half-full perspective has to do with population growth and the demands for goods and services. As global fertility rates will likely continue to drop (as discussed in *Let's All Learn to Fish*), future labor shortages are distinctly possible. RoPa will help plug any labor gaps so that the demands from an aging population can still be met. There's more: Did you know that there are firms which have been executing on RoPa and have seen job creation from it?[108] Just imagine updating the

---

106 Daniel Dennett, "Will AI achieve consciousness? Wrong question," *Wired* (Feb. 2, 2019), https://
www.wired.com/story/will-ai-achieve-consciousness-wrong-question/

107 David Rotman and Iain Cockburn, "AI is reinventing the way we invent," *MIT Technology Review*
(Feb. 15, 2019), https://www.technologyreview.com/s/612898/ai-is-reinventing-the-way-we-invent

108 Michael Koch, Ilya Manuylov, and Marcel Smolka, "Robots and firms," *VOX* (July 1, 2019), https://
voxeu.org/article/robots-and-firms

Republican Party's 1928 promise of "a chicken in every pot and a car in every backyard" with a robot (worker) in every household!

Let's agree, if robots were to be leveraged as and respected as helpful tools, which they are, then RoPa! It's Us and Them.

*I've come up with a set of rules that describe
our reactions to technologies:*

*Anything that is in the world when you're born is normal and
ordinary and is just a natural part of the way the world works.*

*Anything that's invented between when you're fifteen
and thirty-five is new and exciting and revolutionary
and you can probably get a career in it.*

*Anything invented after you're thirty-five is
against the natural order of things.*

–Douglas Adams, from The Salmon of Doubt *(2002)*

Chapter 4:
Income for Everyone?

"[T]here can be no doubt that some minimum of food,

shelter, and clothing, sufficient to preserve health and

the capacity to work, can be assured to everybody ... Nor

is there any reason why the state should not assist the

individual in providing for those common hazards of life

against which, because of their uncertainty, few individuals

can make adequate provision."

—Friedrich Hayek[109]

My first book was largely about rethinking entitlements that are no longer affordable and are a threat to sustaining or increasing today's productivity levels. This closing chapter in my follow-up book concludes with what many could consider a huge entitlement: Universal Basic Income ... *huh*? There are two keys to why I think this apparent contradiction is more than okay: HALTsi[110] (mentioned in *Let's All Learn to Fish*), and the barbelling of work (mentioned in chapter 3 of this book). Let's understand the two key reasons why I argue that a UBI would be helpful.

The first reason is that HALTsi negatively affects decision-making. Although any of the six states denoted by "HALTsi" can be triggered in a multitude of ways, poverty "instigates" the first four states and increases the risks of the last two. The linkages of the first four to poverty are both clear and significant. Now consider how poverty

---

[109] *The Road to Serfdom* (Routledge, 1944), pp. 148–149.

[110] The psychological research has referred to HALT (hungry, angry, lonely, or tired) for years; my "si" for sick or injured has long needed to be added, in my humble opinion.

drives a scarcity mindset. As economist Sendhil Mullainathan and psychologist Eldar Shafir wrote, "This mindset [of scarcity] brings two benefits. It concentrates the mind on pressing needs. It also gives people a keener sense of the value of a dollar, minute, calorie, or smile … . [But] this scarcity mindset can also be debilitating. It shortens a person's horizons and narrows his perspective, creating a dangerous tunnel vision. Anxiety also saps brainpower and willpower, reducing mental bandwidth."[111]

These types of impacts on brainpower can lead to "a drop in cognitive function similar to a 13-point dip in IQ, or the loss of an entire night's sleep."[112] When you consider that an average IQ is 90 110, a 13-point dip is equivalent to roughly a 15% drop in intelligence. If the drop causes IQ to drop below 80, that's where cognitive deficiencies become visible and noticeable. This can happen to a person who is otherwise in the range of average intelligence. Two questions: (1) If everyone was able to use more of their own brainpower, how much additional productivity might the country receive (what might the $56,000 figure rise to)? and (2) If more and more people experience brainpower "outages" more often, then what would the cost be to society?

It's not HALTsi, but Daniel Kahneman's (2002 Nobel Laureate in Economics) Princeton study on "Can money buy happiness?"[113] seems connected. What the researchers learned was that making little money did not cause sadness in and of itself, but it did tend to heighten and exacerbate existing worries. For example, among people who were divorced, 51% of those who made less than $1,000 per month reported having felt sad or stressed the previous day, whereas that number fell to 24% among those earning more than $3,000 per month. Having more money seems to provide those undergoing adversity with greater security and resources for dealing with their troubles.

The barbelling of work has begun and will likely continue to contribute to a relative increase in the number of jobs with lower pay as compared to those that were considered more middle class in the past. To what extent this will increase aspects of HALTsi, or HALTsi's impacts, is not knowable. However, longer breaks in employment (lags) and lower pay possess a potential to increase HALTsi. And, as barbelling becomes bigger, the impacts will likely be realized.[114] Whether there's a genuine push of many

---

[111] Sendhil Mullainathan and Eldar Shafir, *Scarcity: Why Having Too Little Means So Much* (Times Books/Henry Holt, 2013).

[112] Morgan Kelly, "Poor concentration: Poverty reduces brainpower needed for navigating other areas of life," Princeton University (Aug. 29, 2013), https://www.princeton.edu/news/2013/08/29/poor-concentration-poverty-reduces-brainpower-needed-navigating-other-areas-life

[113] Daniel Kahneman and Angus Deaton, "High income improves evaluation of life but not emotional well-being," *PNAS* 107(38) 16489–16493 (Sept. 21, 2010), https://doi.org/10.1073/pnas.1011492107

[114] The "A" for angry/anger (crying out for help?) seems to be a factor in more and more (geo)politics and the growing expressions of nationalism, for example.

into poverty versus just *toward* poverty, the potential for hardship is real because of pre-existing lifestyles and liabilities, with the corresponding expenses that may no longer be affordable. While an initial thought might be simply "cut back," that may not be so easy for a primary expense like a home. Can the home be sold in order to downsize?[115] Will the next home be that much cheaper? What might a new commute to work cost?

Also, who is going to be a buyer if the "higher-paying jobs" are limited in the area? Keep in mind that dominant employers, the primary buyers of labor in an area, have more pricing power over labor.[116] Now, I don't know of any existing data or research that indicates a significant or increasing push of people toward poverty who aren't already coping with financial hardships. Nevertheless, today's so-called "have not's" may not have very much room to cut their spending in order to accommodate a pay cut as a result of the barbelling of work, and the changes to work that may be coming.

Finally, although the "barbell" label is a wonderful metaphor for the varying pay levels, it could overcolor the future in that it describes an equal balance between high- and low-paying work. An unbalanced barbell, overweighted toward low-paying jobs, is also possible while high-priced essential goods and services such as healthcare exist.

The more people experience lower-paying jobs and incidences of HALTsi, the more trust in society and capitalism[117] will be diminished. Furthermore, those different from "Us" will be judged unfairly and tribalism will rise, politics will become more polarized, and society will begin to pull apart: "Lower levels of trust among minorities and low-income groups are in sync with a pattern that scholars have long observed—people who feel vulnerable or disadvantaged, for whatever reason, tend to find it riskier to trust because they're less well-fortified to deal with the consequences of misplaced trust."[118]

Where are we today? Maybe too near the intersection of fear and anger? This is where it gets difficult. People need to work toward owning their fears and anger and try to understand what underlies those feelings. Without delving into psychology—which is

---

[115] This challenge was very much an issue during the Great Recession of 2008–09.

[116] Also, monopsony isn't subject to potential antitrust actions by a justice department, as monopolies are.

[117] Although capitalism seems to have stumbled, it has not fallen and still remains the best "ism" the world has ever known: *best* as in having lifted more people out of poverty than any other system ever attempted, including socialism. Nevertheless, capitalism's rules can be improved with newer ideas (such as those in chapter 1) and rise again to be better, and more inclusive, than ever.

[118] Pamela Paxton, "Trust in decline?" *Contexts* 4(1): 40–46 (2015); see also Robert Wuthnow, "The foundations of trust," *Philosophy & Public Policy Quarterly* 18(3): 3–8 (1998).

beyond the scope of this book—today sees unemployment in the 4%[119] neighborhood, hourly wages rising, and little to no headline inflation.

So, why so fearful, why so angry? Perhaps you are one of those not participating or participating to the extent you think you *should* be in this reasonably strong economy. Can you take responsibility and improve your situation? Taking responsibility in this context may mean upskilling; it does not mean blaming others or turning to nationalism. Do you have a view, an opinion, that the country owes you something?[120] If so, can you understand that this perspective is an entitlement mentality? Do you understand that the fear or anger often underlying or producing those emotions is not healthy? You can choose *not* to be a victim (remember "the pleasure at being the cause" with work?) and know that society does have a vested interest in helping you. After all, a society with more trust is more cohesive and stronger. To move away from victimhood, begin to work toward an understanding of how you can pursue what you want. A new or better job may require upskilling or better people skills, and will require at least an investment in time, if not both time and money. A new or better (personal) spending plan along with improved financial literacy might also be helpful in reducing your stress.

Societies can't simply give high-paying jobs to everyone; societies don't have them. After all, where would all these good jobs come from, and why would we assume that everyone would be fully capable of doing them? An offer of cash in lieu of a job could be a better route and could be easier, but societies would need to "find" that money. How much money is made available depends on what kind of "end of HALTsi" (EoH) platform society wants to support. The platform should be sturdy enough to support those who are upskilling by giving them time, at a minimum, and perhaps strong enough to augment hourly wages or replace lost hours. Because we can't know all who need support today or will need support in the future, the platform would have to be available to everyone. Please recognize that the EoH platform must promote productivity; productivity is how an EoH platform can be made sustainable.

A UBI has what could make for a good EoH platform. In my opinion, UBI could be a tremendous trampoline (remember safety nets *and* trampolines?) for the majority of people. Consider, for a moment, a few of the potential societal "returns" from a UBI:

---

[119] Thinking of U3 in the United States as of Spring 2019, it was 3.6% and thus nearly about the historical 4% rate we seem to return to time and time again. A different view is the labor force participation rate—because to be unemployed you must be a participant, and today's participation rate is about 63%. Since WWII, the lowest has been 58% and the highest 67%, but our population is much bigger today. 63% is not that good.

[120] I think we should accept entitled mentalities—to an extent—if only from those who have served in and seen action in our military (they gave, we owe), and children (you're the reason they're here).

less crime due to fewer unmet basic needs and the connections that has to better decision-making; lower healthcare costs due to less stress and higher productivity, likely as a result from opportunity equality; maybe even an increase in work hours—more productivity from those already employed who can now afford more childcare; and so on. Extra income for those with little can be life-changing!

In theory, UBI is brilliant, but what about in practice? Are there any other platforms that might be able to do the job as well? Is UBI the answer to what ails us?

In practice...

We must first define the *U* and the *B* of a UBI. What's *universal*? Is this everyone, or a subset? For example, a subset could be all adults, who are citizens, and who are over the age of 18, 21, or 25, and … etcetera. What about kids—those working versus unemployed—and how about covering everyone versus just those below an income threshold? In short, just how universal should Universal be? Defining *basic* is equally tough; the B could be the poverty level rounded to the nearest hundred dollars or higher or lower. What about the B varying due to varying costs of living in different regions/states?[121] Each different dimension alters the cost of UBI, changes the ability to offer it at all, and could impact the motivations of its recipients. To date, many UBI designs would grant all adult citizens above the age of 18 a stipend of $1,000 per month (which is roughly 2018's U.S. poverty level) and with children too but at $500 per month per child. The cost of a UBI is ground zero for taking the theory and putting it into practice.

As a replacement of all social insurance programs, UBI is *not* a good idea. Programs that leverage large numbers of people to socialize large unexpected, individual costs simply cannot be replaced without greater costs when insurance programs are shifted to individuals rather than across many people. Social Security's retirement benefits are a great example of how those who live longer benefit from those who die prematurely and would have to remain unchanged (but could be improved, as discussed in *Let's All Learn to Fish*). Another great example is healthcare, which subsidizes the costs of those who are sick using payments from those who are healthy and not currently in need of healthcare. Although a UBI would undoubtedly help people cover healthcare costs, the current U.S. system would easily eat up most of any UBI payments for too many people. In my prior book, I proposed an approach to curing healthcare (see chapter 3 of *Let's All Learn to Fish*); Dr. Carolyn McClanahan has also written about a

---

[121] This could have good or bad consequences; I prefer one B and let people relocate as they wish based on potential work opportunities or lower living expenses.

solution[122] that has very interesting potential. With either of the two healthcare solutions, the answer is a benefit that's separate from employment due to the potential increased number of self-employed and gig-workers in the future (with or without UBI) and to help free people from jobs they're keeping solely for the access to healthcare benefits. Before any UBI can be set up, *healthcare must be cured, be accessible and affordable for all*.

What about motivations? Apart from the cost of a UBI, concerns about "buying complacency" is the biggest worry. Although no UBI trial, out of many, has resulted in a decline in work, no trial has been big enough or long enough in duration to put an end to this worry. We can explore, however, why a UBI at or below a poverty level might cause less work to be done. Let's think about it:

- Some people might reduce their hours of paid work (to take it easier), but wouldn't other part-timers or those who are unemployed fill that open time … especially if hours, jobs, and work are difficult to obtain? However, there seems to be no shortage of work[123] to be done across the United States, if only to satisfy our infrastructure needs.
- Some people might reduce their hours or discontinue their paid work to help more at home or through volunteer efforts. These types of stoppages are beneficial to others. Please slow down and recognize that not all work that is good work is paid work.
- Some people might reduce their hours or discontinue their paid work to go back to school, learn a new skill, or start a business. This type of work stoppage would be temporary before "unlocking" future productivity improvements.

Of course, some unemployed people would choose to remain unemployed, but that would not cause a drop in aggregate productivity. Regardless, their HALTsi would be alleviated.

In addition, minimum-wage laws might no longer be necessary. In fact, wages could even rise, if employers needed to fill vacant jobs as a result of some people staying out or holding out because they can be pickier about their work and pay or because their own entrepreneurial thoughts and efforts are stoked.

---

[122] Carolyn McClanahan, "Politicians need to change the conversation on how to fix health care," *Forbes* (Jan. 28, 2018), https://www.forbes.com/sites/carolynmcclanahan/2018/01/28/politicians-need-to-change-the-conversation-on-how-to-fix-health-care/#9b812c16caeb

[123] Rather, there's a shortage of good policies and economic decisions on how and where money is spent.

As a reminder from chapter 2, don't underestimate the importance of work and self-esteem to people. This is so even if some people do not wish to self-actualize themselves all the way to the top of Maslow's pyramid.

With a UBI, immigration challenges would likely increase, with more people wanting to come to the United States. A durable, functional immigration solution is needed (UBI or not). **Solve this policy challenge** first or suffer greater immigration challenges and the heightened partisan politics that result.

Then again … Let's pause and ask if there is that much HALTsi going on, and whether so many jobs have been lost to automation that we do in fact need to talk about UBI. With people in or near poverty, yes, HALTsi is going on, though to what extent may be impossible to measure accurately. Nevertheless, its existence absolutely makes getting out of or away from poverty tougher. Rich, developed, countries need to look in the mirror and ask how much, if any, poverty should be acceptable. Why? Because poverty is not about a lack of character—as it has been said—but about a lack of money. GOT THAT?! In fact, there's interesting behavioral research[124] which shows that these alleged character flaws in fact produce quality decision-making: when money does come in (a positive wealth shock), the "sub-prime" group pays down debt and reduces revolving credit balances. When it comes to job losses, despite all the fearmongering estimates of a robot apocalypse, only a small fraction of the upwards-of-60%-loss estimates have actually been lost (so far). Yes, jobs may be lost gradually and then suddenly,[125] but only time will tell. Regardless, the time to buy fire insurance is before the fire. Remember, there's plenty of work available today that's not even being done—U.S. infrastructure, personal healthcare assistance—that could aid productivity with both the work and the improved infrastructure.

Interestingly, those currently on benefits would lose out, says the OECD, especially in countries where existing social protection is comprehensive.[126] They think that the rich and the poor would gain the least, whereas people on middle incomes would gain the most. Early retirees also stand to lose out. A couple of thoughts for the OECD: I'm not sure a lot of people care about the rich not gaining; the poor would only lose to the extent that integration with other protections is not done thoughtfully (so that they don't lose); a better-off middle class is just good; and early retirement is

---

[124] J. Anthony Cookson, Erik P. Gilje, and Rawley Z. Heimer, "Shale shocked: The long run effect of wealth on household debt" (n.d.), http://gattonweb.uky.edu/faculty/hankins/conf2019/shale.pdf

[125] Thank you for this fun perspective, Mr. Hemingway.

[126] World Economic Forum, "Universal basic income is gaining support—but could it make poverty worse?" (June 15, 2017), https://medium.com/world-economic-forum/universal-basic-income-is-gaining-support-but-could-it-make-poverty-worse-3ff62c64608

not helpful to productivity anyway. Nevertheless, the OECD was on point when they demonstrated concern about the cost of a UBI program, and the importance of how it's specifically designed.

Other EoH types of platforms (trampolines)

Let's briefly review some other UBI-styled alternatives that may be worthy of consideration.

Negative income taxes

This is an old idea that dates to the 1940s; the idea is that people below a certain level of income receive supplemental income from the government in lieu of paying taxes. It's a simple approach that can conquer poverty for those who are working. Could this be made to apply to those who are unable to work or below the poverty threshold? It seems very much so. While there are many benefit programs in existence already, a UBI would seem to be much more efficient[127] and possibly even cost less overall due to "everyone in" and no conditionality for receipt. Consider the following:

> … ran the numbers and concluded that for the combined cost of the earned income tax credit, Supplemental Security Income, food stamps, cash welfare, school meal programs, and housing subsidies, you could fund a negative income tax at poverty-line levels … you could swap out those programs, put a guaranteed income in their place, and wipe out poverty entirely.[128]

What's interesting about that anti-poverty work is that it essentially proposes a UBI, but solely for those in poverty—a narrowly defined U versus a U that includes everyone. Maybe that would be better; it would dramatically lower the overall cost and raise the practicality. However, this wouldn't help those who lose material income—are "underemployed"—but not yet in or near poverty. The question is how well improved unemployment and lifelong learning programs could integrate and offset the risks to those individuals. *If UBI is NOT aligning with people's "belief" systems or imagined to be too costly, then negative income taxes should be pursued as THE EoH platform. And, while it can and will eradicate poverty, the negative stigma[129] of poverty would likely remain.*

---

[127] The cost of verifying the need—qualifying for a B—would be significant.

[128] Jessica Wiederspan, Elizabeth Rhodes, and H. Luke Shaefer, "Expanding the discourse on antipoverty policy: Reconsidering a negative income tax," *Journal of Poverty* 19(2), 218–238 (2015). doi:10.1080/10875549.2014.991889, https://www.tandfonline.com/doi/full/10.1080/10875549.2014.991889#abstract

[129] Can stigmas be of value? Though this may seem an odd question due to the negative connotation of the word, comfort with bad, unfortunate circumstances seems odd, too.

Earned income tax credit (EITC)

In the U.S. tax code, there's a "refundable" credit available—that is, cash—if you earn less than "x" based on your tax filing status and number of children. This is essentially a small-scale negative income tax for those who are eligible and claim it. However, it requires both employment income and action by the worker. If this is of any interest, then it would seem better to pursue an outright negative income tax, because it's simpler. Simple is better because people would simply receive the benefit of a negative income tax rather than having to "apply" for it with their tax filing. Simple makes failing harder to do.

Baby bonds

These are interesting, but only if as a trampoline for the next generation. This idea, as the name implies, applies to just babies. While this idea could begin, it would take at least one generation to have complete coverage—it cannot help adults today. Also, we should ask if it could be better to spend such dollars to fund quality pre-K and kindergarten, as discussed earlier in this book. Here's the idea:

> A trust account for every newborn of up to $60,000 dollars (average $25,000, minimum of $500), calibrated to the wealth of the family in which they are born. I'm talking about an endowment. Personal seed capital, a publicly established baby trust, what my colleague William Darity at Duke University and I have referred to as baby bonds, a term that was coined by the late historian from Columbia University, Manning Marable ... 2% guaranteed interest and available at reaching adulthood.[130]

Again, an interesting idea—but pre-K and kindergarten may provide much more bang for the opportunity equality bucks spent. Also, this couldn't serve as a replacement for a UBI: it fails on the U.

GDP dividends

Though intriguing, these are not likely to be a sturdy enough trampoline. A GDP dividend is a per-head, flat-percentage-share dollar amount determined annually and then distributed to citizens as their "dividend" in what the country produced in the prior year. What's most intriguing about this idea is that it could help everyone feel like a part of the whole, result in some thinking about their role, and promote overall inclusivity as well as always being affordable because it's based on GDP. However relatively small to a B, it would still have to be paid by the government. Conceptually,

---

[130] Darrick Hamilton, "How baby bonds could help close the wealth gap," TED talk (Dec. 12, 2018), https://www.ted.com/talks/darrick_hamilton_how_baby_bonds_could_help_close_the_wealth_gap/transcript?utm_source=newsletter_weekly_2018-12-22&utm_campaign=newsletter_week-ly&utm_medium=email&utm_content=bottom_right_image

it's not very different from a UBI except for the smaller B and the variability year-to-year, which could be problematic for those in poverty.

A "revenue share for all"

Yes, let's. However, this is for businesses/employees and not a trampoline as such for everyone. What if the relationship between capital (employers) and labor (employees) could shift toward a more elegant solution[131] that improves trust (through transparency), helps with unequal pay (by supplying a clear basis and specifying how it could change) and likely generates greater productivity via a greater ownership—not entitlement—mentality? Figure 17 shows a breakdown of the idea.

Figure 17. Revenue share for everyone? Yes, really!

Firm Net Income w/o Compensation:	$X,XXX,XXX
Firm Investment Account:	Minus 5 – 10%
Money for Firm's Talent:	$X,XXX,XXX
Fixed Allocation % to Equity Pool:	10%? Hurdle?
Revenue Share Pool for All!!!:	Defined by Role

Adjustments can be made for: Behaviors (=/-), Net sales efforts (=/-) …

- Investment account = a potential capital account (reserves, investment dollars, for dividend or interest payments)
- Equity pool = a form of a dividend for owners, perhaps with a hurdle before it's allowed to be paid out
- Revenue Share pool = the compensation pool (salary and bonus) that is shared by all employees and varies by role/responsibility level. Because many employees don't enjoy paychecks that vary from check to check, the Revenue Share pool could be reduced by the amount of fixed or base salaries, only to remain for bonuses
- Adjustments, if any, would be made at the individual level and be reallocated into or from the pool.

This can't be a trampoline because it only works for those who are working. However, the potential benefits of the clarity—even with the unequal payments—of this approach could constitute a very positive change for employees and reduce the capital-versus-labor issues.

---

[131] This is the author's concept, which I have discussed with some clients in the course of my colleagues' and my work.

Now theory *and* practice[132]

First and foremost, how could we pay for a UBI type of trampoline? It's a nonstarter if we can't afford it. Let's also hope for only very minor unintended consequences of erecting such a trampoline (ha!—hope is *not* a strategy). After we estimate UBI's gross cost, we need to decide on the social insurance programs UBI could replace in order to estimate its net cost. Then, in the final step, we should try to estimate UBI's returns: that is, the potential pro-growth[133] impacts of the UBI. In this third and final step, the returns are arguably too difficult to predict. Let's consider a design with the following attributes (we must start somewhere!).

- The U should *not* be "universal" because it needs to be a trampoline rather than a safety net:
  - Age 18 plus having achieved a 12th-grade diploma, a GED equivalent, or an accepted[134] vocational "certificate," whichever comes last.
  - A benefit equal to 50% of the adult U benefit would be provided to young kids—specifically, kids from birth until they reach 40 months old (or rounded up to four years to simplify)—to act as a *huge* boost to their health and opportunity equality.[135] While some UBI schemes propose to extend benefits to age 18, which is not a bad idea, I hesitate to make that part of my initial U, mainly because of the cost impact and a little concern about the possible incentive for people to have more kids for the money rather than desire to be a parent. However, a "complete" benefit could very well make sense if affordable.
  - UBI payments would *not* be included in a worker's income used to determine Social Security retirement income benefits.

- The B—for the basic benefit—would be:
  - $833 per month ($10,000 per year), rather than the often-discussed $1,000 per month. This would help to minimize HALTsi in the same manner and would lower the gross cost of a UBI. This amount simulates an hourly boost of $5 per hour (across 2,000 hours of full-time work), so it's a big percentage boost to current

---

132 Because "In theory there is no difference between theory and practice. In practice there is" said by Yogi Berra among others. And, the practice numbers used are U.S. data.

133 Michalis Nikiforos, Marshall Steinbaum, and Gennaro Zezza, *Modeling the Macroeconomic Effects of a Universal Basic Income* (Roosevelt Institute, Aug. 2017), http://rooseveltinstitute.org/wp-content/uploads/2017/08/Modeling-the-Macroeconomic-Effects-of-a-Universal-Basic-Income.pdf

134 In the United States, each state could compile a list based on employers' surveys of sought-after skills or skill gaps. This list would qualify. All other certificates could challenge to be accepted.

135 Kimberly Noble, "How does income affect childhood brain development?" TED talk (Apr. 6, 2019), https://www.ted.com/talks/kimberly_noble_how_does_income_affect_childhood_brain_development/discussion?utm_source=newsletter_weekly_2019-04-06&utm_campaign=newsletter_weekly&utm_medium=email&utm_content=talk_of_the_week_button#t-452338

hourly worker rates. Oddly coincidental, $10,000 happens to fit with TLR Analytics' 2012 U.S. data and illustration of a $10,000 slip[136] from trend (see Figure 18).

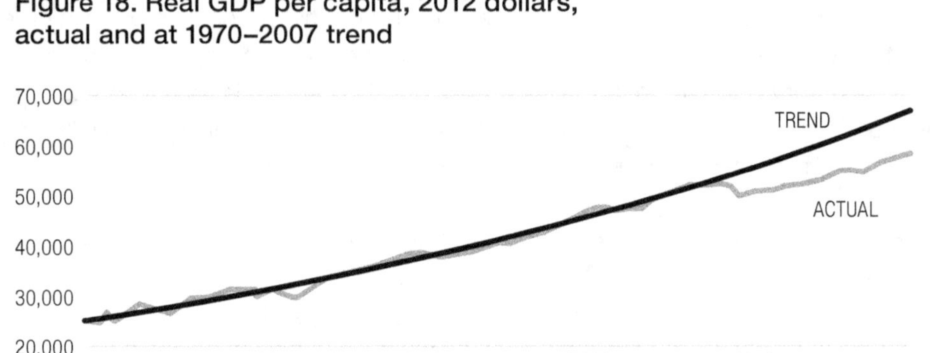

Figure 18. Real GDP per capita, 2012 dollars, actual and at 1970–2007 trend

Please keep in mind that help is important—but so are incentives to work; this is an attempt to help but not too much. In the future, this amount could always be increased if deemed necessary and affordable; future amounts could also be indexed to inflation. But we want, we need people to work.

This makes this author think about the FIRE (financial independence, retire early) movement. This amount could, in fact, help someone to (try to) retire early—and the potential loss of all that productivity is disturbing. But the FIRE movement may flame out. In fact, a "Barista FIRE" movement (classic FIRE, but working part-time to cover health insurance costs) has started, arguably to be more realistic until or unless the U.S. healthcare system is cured. Aside from Barista FIRE, stories of gaming the healthcare system and "borrowing" Netflix passwords or Amazon Prime accounts were popular … maybe they need to spend more than they claim. Regardless, if people wish to live on much less of an income, it's laudable and their own decision. I remain skeptical.

Implementation

A monthly debit card would be issued to all U-citizens and available for pickup, in-person. This card would be electronically refilled monthly.

All debit-card spending would be recorded in a searchable format and made available for open-source research (but no more granular than a zip code) and understanding of the spending.

---

[136] Hmm, we can't really be entitled to a smooth, upward trend. That's why I used the word "coincidentally."

With a better understanding of spending, incentives could be considered for what are deemed pro-social or "healthy" spending choices. For example, an incentive could be to debit the card for less than the full price at the point of purchase for pro-social or healthy items. Although this would be positive "nudging," I have no illusions that getting universal agreement on such incentives would be easy.

The cost is … possibly too affordable to ignore. Furthermore, if a UBI would, could, increase productivity, then we would *want* to afford it because the increased productivity would help to cover (justify) the expense. If a UBI would—and it would—help minimize HALTsi or help maximize opportunity equality, then why wouldn't we want to afford UBI? So, let's get to work and find the money for UBI; think from theory to practice. Here's an estimate of its affordability based on a gross estimated cost of about $2.35 trillion dollars per year[137] and some tax modifications in the United States considering the current population demographics for adults and children and providing just the first four years as the benefit for children.

The **offsetting cost savings** of reduced welfare benefits[138] from various UBI proponents has been estimated to be in the range of $1.0–$1.5 trillion per year. While these estimates could be overoptimistic, the numbers do seem reasonable to this author. Keep in mind that a big proportion (upwards of 50%) of the reduction in welfare benefits comes from reducing pension and Social Security payments equal to the UBI.

Helpful taxes

An **annual wealth** tax for the 0.1% is estimated to produce $200 billion per year over the next 10 years. As mentioned earlier in the book, this could help society's cohesion in addition to helping fund a UBI. And, who knows if other wealthy individuals—along the lines of the Gates pledge—just might be okay with contributing to a sequestered fund?

A **land tax**, if instituted for businesses, is estimated to produce "x", potentially a BIG number. Then again, per my first book, I wondered why we couldn't have a minimum tax regardless of deductions for businesses with profits.[139] This would certainly be a sizable positive "if," but should only be counted as an unknown, just as above.

---

[137] To get $2.35 trillion, it's U.S. adults (225 million of us at $10,000 each) plus U.S. children aged 0–4 (20 million at $5,000 each). If the B was the "typical" $12,000 per year, and all children 0–18 were at 50%, then the cost would be $3.55 trillion. I think this makes for a good low-to-high range.

[138] Now consider: if there's no "cost" to working because of discontinued welfare benefits, then more work would/could be expected with UBI.

[139] Although this could seem very attractive, it would require further definition to avoid ensnaring good, ethical accounting and investing by businesses.

A **carbon tax**—I mean, come on, it's the least we could do[140] for our planet—could easily raise at least $150 billion but may not be sustainable (ha-ha) if carbon usage drops materially.[141] By the way, rising temperatures and oceans which lead to nastier weather globally furthers opportunity inequality since those living in les developed global area/regions often have fewer financial abilities to be resilient.

And, regular taxation of the UBI if the average tax take is 17% (in the middle of the 12% and 22% 2019 marginal brackets) is $400 billion per year. I have not tinkered with the tax code to garner any other assistance.

Other **potential gains** (apart from all the positives for people) would also appear:

- The savings from less crime, reduced usage of the courts, and significant reduction in the cost of running prisons has been estimated at up to $200 billion per year.
- The UBI would most likely get spent (don't forget that). The result would be more spending, which means economic growth,[142] and more taxes would result from that growth—estimated at "x."
- Curing healthcare, a first-order issue before allowing a UBI, would produce savings of "x."

The conclusion is that a UBI appears to be affordable because the cost exceeds the "known" offsets or expected revenues by an estimated amount of at most $400 billion (using $1.0 trillion, the bottom end of the savings estimates). This is less than 2% of the more than $20 trillion U.S. GDP. The estimated $400 billion cost also doesn't figure in any economic growth, land taxes, minimum corporate taxes, or a wealth tax for the top 0.X%, due to their "iffy-ness." UBI is (or can be) affordable, and it would be helpful for many people and could seemingly put an end to poverty.

---

[140] "The least" because a proper incentive is easier (and arguably more effective) than suggesting diets of less fossil fuel consumption and the related societal costs. However, how big a tax would be effective and how large could it be before other, serious unintended consequences appear? Both questions are beyond the scope of this book, but we must start somewhere. Maybe a gradual, rising tax would promote behavior changes and technological development before the tax costs produce unintended consequences. Although this cannot solve the global issue, the United States can certainly take responsibility for its share.

[141] Can you imagine how largw scale 3D printing could reverse globalization and how that could help aside from many other wide-ranging impacts?

[142] Which, for example, PwC forecasts as being worth roughly $16 trillion globally by 2030; this is arguably conservative with a global GDP of $100 trillion, but it's a forecast. PwC, "2019 AI predictions," https://www.pwc.com/us/en/services/consulting/library/artificial-intelligence-predictions-2019.html. The forecasted U.S gain is $2.5 trillion: see Catherine Clifford, "A $1,000 per month cash handout would grow the economy by $2.5 trillion, new study says," CNBC.com (Aug. 31, 2017), https://www.cnbc.com/amp/2017/08/31/1000-per-month-cash-handout-would-grow-the-economy-by-2-point-5-trillion.html?__twitter_impression=true&fbclid=IwAR0aDotWvE9Hf-W5lSF826q4fZWVDaEEVC2kmbrGin4YoN3jsrPUcfwf7tbo

Recognize that you could not be out of a job or work for an extended period of time and still be able to pay your bills because of the UBI. The UBI is *not* an answer to mass unemployment challenges … and maybe that's a good thing. We need those who are able to work, to work; it's their productivity that makes the economy better for all of us. What UBI does is ease those periods without work or with less work and enable more peace of mind while looking for work or training to enable better work. So, UBI is *not* the end-all or be-all; it can't be. What UBI can be is a platform to end HALTsi, to help to lift up one side of the barbell and provide a launch pad. It is what's needed. To help stave off harsh consequences of potential mass unemployment challenges, upskilling and retraining have to be made policy priorities. Ideas discussed in earlier chapters, such as corporations paying one-third of their automation savings into local retraining facilities, digital taxes[143] for funding such facilities, and better use of vocational schools generally, among other ideas,[144] need to become reality. With an EoH platform—that is, UBI—safety nets could become less needed and less used, and the stronger trampolines would propel people higher.

To put a finishing point on income for everyone (or at least my U definition), consider the history of means-tested welfare spending shown in Figure 19.

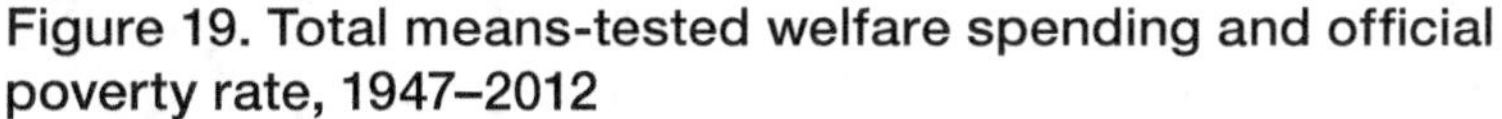

Figure 19. Total means-tested welfare spending and official poverty rate, 1947–2012

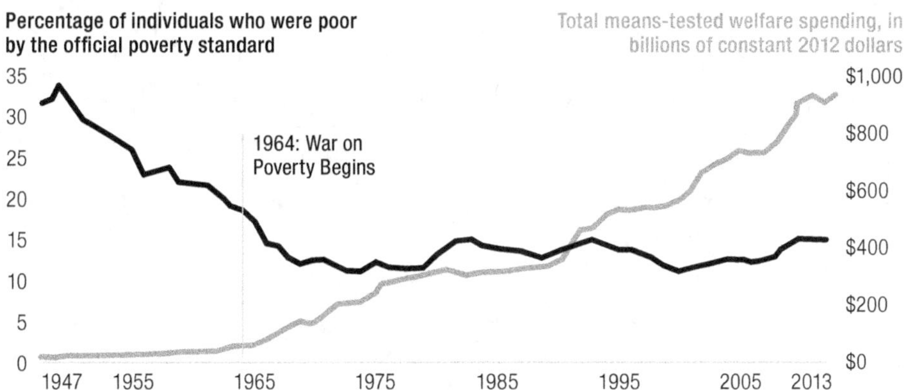

Sources: Poverty figures for 1947–1958: Gordon Fisher, "Estimates of the Poverty Population Under the Current Official Definition for Years Before 1959," U.S. Department of Health and Human Services, Office of the Assistant Secretary for Planning and Evaluation, 1986. Poverty figures for 1959 2012: U.S. Census Bureau, Current Population Survey, Annual Social and Economic Supplements. "Historical Poverty Tables–People," Table 2, https://www.census.gov/hhes/www/poverty/data/historical/people.html. Means-tested welfare spending figures: Heritage Foundation research, U.S. Office of Management and Budget.

---

[143] Based on "society's data" for society's development.

[144] In *Let's All Learn to Fish*, I spoke about making college affordable and better, public/private partnerships, and more. Upskilling and retraining are critical, but so is getting young adults off to better starts.

What we can see is that 10–15% of the population being defined as poor has been a hard barrier to reduce no matter how much money has been spent. This leads me to ask many questions, but here are just two:

- Of these 10–15%, how many are incapable or unwilling to improve their situation? Those who are incapable need safety nets, whereas those who are unwilling need different form(s) of intervention.
- Could spending the money differently, as with a UBI, help? More generally, when all else has been ineffective or stopped making progress, why wouldn't we try?

> *"We cannot solve our problems with the same thinking we used when we created them."*
>
> —Albert Einstein

My Closing

*"The problem is that capitalists typically don't know
how to divide the pie well and socialists typically
don't know how to grow it well."*

—Ray Dalio[145]

Growing the pie requires work, productivity, and innovation, which in turn requires creativity with a dash of audacity. But work also brings many positives that come from the pleasure of being the cause, such as dignity, pride, and self-esteem. Work is good. Dividing the pie requires appreciation that not everyone is able to work and that perhaps they should not be labeled as (fill in the blank). However, those who can work need to work to provide for everyone. When everyone has opportunity equality—the ability to compete in a fair game—we all win. There will be more winners simply because when everyone's "in," more (and different things, too) will be accomplished.

Improved governance plus a UBI platform from which to launch are just what the doctor ordered. The doctor? Yeah: recall how psychologists think about HALT(si) and how it can negatively affect decision-making and behavior more generally. With a UBI-style platform that combines elements of both a safety net and a trampoline, we can begin to minimize failures to launch or relaunch fast enough (in the case of a new job or career). The platform, along with wider/better opportunities to prepare for work via improvements to academic schools and curricula, and a newfound respect for the value of vocational schools, are all necessary. With these and better governance, society can become more cohesive and wealthier than ever. Who wouldn't want *that*?

---

[145] Bridgewater® Daily Observations, April 5, 2019.

Let's choose this new **ERA** and lose our **E**ntitled mentalities to take **R**esponsibility and **A**ppreciate those who need assistance. To help lose our entitled employment mentalities, it may help to come face-to-face with them, because, in all candor, we may not even recognize their existence in ourselves. Here are a couple of examples that might help.

Modifying an old sex joke for an offer of work (of a very different type):

> Employer to prospective employee: Would you "work" for me for $150 per hour?

> Prospective employee: Sure! Yes!

> Employer: Okay, then how about for $15 per hour?

> Prospective employee: What do you think I am?

> Employer: We've already established what you are; all we're doing now is bargaining about your wages.

Not so funny (ever?).

And for you employers (or entrepreneurs) out there, you only *think* that you're your own boss. Hello? You have clients. Why should anyone do business with you or hire you? What should buyers pay for your goods or services (how do you value your business or value yourself)?

Bottom line: We all work for other people until and unless we're retired or incapable of working.

Almost everyone has some entitlement tendencies, whether it's about how much you "should" be paid or in some other aspect of your life (hint—watch people's behavior in airports to see it live and in color). The first step is to admit to what extent you're entitled. Now you can benefit from attempting to understand what about and why. Then … STOP IT! The world doesn't owe us anything; it was here long before we arrived and will be here long after we're gone. Regardless, we can *choose* to owe each other—our fellow humans. After all, collaboration/cooperation is how we came to dominate all other species on this planet. We need each other, as many able people as possible, to take responsibility to improve governance and the aggregate productivity that affects everyone. Imagine what would happen to that $56,000 average income if we increased that year's average number of productive work hours per day from three to six (still 25% less than the storied eight-hour workday that very few people actually experience).[146] The new average income of $112,000 would go a very long way toward improving everyone's well-being. Imagine again, but this time for how much "not wanting" for life's basics could become a reality. Appreciate all that would result, whether an individual is able or unable to work.

Opportunity equality begins early; it's helped by not living in extreme poverty, having access to basic education, becoming literate, being vaccinated, living in a democracy, and surviving to the age of 5. With appreciation of this "Big 5," people of this world have never been better off.[147] However, when we focus our sights on the United States—a wealthy country—many if not all these aspects are considered "should haves." Hello again? That's an entitled mentality. It's not that a wealthy country couldn't have all these elements of opportunity equality; rather, it's about how we're prioritizing their importance and our willingness to make "basics" universally available. The basics—covered in *Let's All Learn to Fish*—are consistent nutrition, access to quality education, and safe/stable environments.[148] With young children, these three basics promote brain growth at the most critical time, which cannot be made up for or regained later. With an addition of access to affordable, quality healthcare, we could argue that children and adults alike would have all their basics covered with a UBI.

Beyond the basics lies the realm of "wanting." It's not that wanting is bad; rather, you should understand that it can be insatiable and lead a "hamster" to never slow down and get off that damn wheel. We all know how bad this is for hamsters, right? The basics allow us to live freely while our wants comfort our ego. Lounge in a warm, soft, cozy "safety net" for too long, and you might not be able to easily get back up and into the economy—leaving you captured by the net instead of boosted by a trampoline. Wanting to win an argument comforts an ego but might alienate co-workers/colleagues if you need to win all the time. Mark Twain told us that "comparison is the death of joy." Comparison is about wants and the "relative" judgments about what we have; for example, driving an expensive Mercedes Benz versus a cost-efficient Chevrolet. Both cars will get you to where you want to go safely, but only the Mercedes is likely to boost your ego. The relative difference is *big*, but the absolute difference is insignificant.

---

[146] Nobel Laureate Daniel Kahneman's lifetime collaborator, Amos Tversky, once said that "the secret to doing good research is always to be a little underemployed. You waste years by not being able to waste hours." Perhaps we would all be a little better-off if not everyone experiences the eight-hour workday—or if the hours worked were productive and not just spent in bullshit jobs.

[147] Max Roser, "The world as 100 people over the last two centuries," *Our World in Data*, https://www. aei.org/wp-content/uploads/2017/07/world-1.jpg

[148] These three aspects of opportunity equality have primacy, and family structure is as much a part of any solution as are the public policies and economics discussed in this and my prior book.

People think and feel in relative (ego), but people begin to live in the absolute (Maslow's bottom two rungs: physiological and safety needs). Wealthy societies could (dare I write "should") afford Maslow's bottom absolutes.

If we become responsible to each other, we will all be able to afford the safety nets and trampolines that enable "not wanting." So, it's with an expectation (or hope) that capitalism will *not* be thrown away in favor of socialism, but rather that it improves and offers more inclusivity. It's capitalism that motivates our productivity, and it's that very productivity that affords what the socialists (and many more people) want: greater dignity for everyone. We need to elevate capitalism from its less than fully appreciated status in many of today's conversations. By the way, it's not that capitalists don't *know* how to divide the pie: they were never charged with the responsibility for doing so. Competition with clear and consistently applied fair rules is supposed to help divide the pie. Chapter 1's focus on governance was about failures or risks given the (un) clarity, (in)consistency, and (un)fairness of our present rules. We can do better.

Let's demand a fair game, with clear rules that apply equally to everyone. Then, if we evolve our thinking to a new ERA, with a UBI, everyone who is capable of playing will be able to play and those who are incapable will at least have dignity—that's inclusiveness. The resulting opportunity equality will broaden and strengthen the "middle"[149] and the economy as a result. A big, strong middle (individual income levels of roughly $40,000 to $120,000) is vital to economic growth because unlike people in poverty or the small number of "rich" people, they are the "marginals" that make all the difference with demand. They are the marginal buyers of most goods and services, because those who are poor can't afford such purchases and the rich don't need to buy that much relative to their income. The middle has the marginal savings that helped make education a goal versus working for the other cohort's kids. And it's the marginal's kids who add the most productivity to society with their education-driven work and goals (yes, some wants are good).

Even if you don't completely agree with the figures used for the middle's income range, you must agree with the simple fact that a UBI will help—push—many people/ households toward the middle and help the economy, which in turn helps everyone. If you consider that such a push toward the middle is unfair, then you must really think that winning and success are solely about hard work rather than work plus luck.[150] Two thoughts: I feel sad for you, and why is that unfair? We can help enable dignity,

---

[149] Let's not confuse "class" (e.g., aspirations, values, beliefs, and behaviors) with "income."
[150] I covered this very directly in chapter 2 of *Let's All Learn to Fish*.

minimize HALTsi, create a more cohesive society. Let's welcome opportunity equality and greater well-being for everyone! Upon achieving *that*, we could begin to reframe well-being away from Maslow's physiological and safety needs and toward something healthier.

In Buddhism:

> Life is/means *Dukkha* (mental dysfunction or suffering)
> Dukkha arises from craving
> Dukkha can be eliminated

Let's minimize craving and enable "not wanting," because not wanting is well-being.

Less HALTsi helps enable well-being (a/k/a happiness). So, let's help enable happiness and … Get to Work … On OUR Future!

The Post-Game

Now that my 2016 fishing expedition is over, is there any better way to say goodbye than with a "Dear John" letter?

Dear John,

Thank you.

If only everyone could just imagine (as you did) and recall your lyrics to "Imagine" (1971). In particular, I'd like to call attention (or is it a call to attention?) a few specific lines:

- *Imagine all the people*
- *Living life in peace*
- *No need for greed or hunger*
- *Sharing all the world*

that were written/sung so beautifully in a way to which I could only aspire ... as I have merely attempted with my books.

*Farewell**

* My hope for everyone, fare thee well … As it turned out, the completion of this book's edits coincided with my receiving a death sentence. On September 26, 2019, I was diagnosed with ALS. Hmm… my post-game includes learned news about a disease made "famous" by Lou Gehrig, a Hall of Fame baseball player. As baseball was my first love, this is not so much poetic as poignant. Goodbye in 3–5 (based on today's available medical treatments.) And, please do NOT feel sorry for me. I have had a good life. My only last wish is for my guiding purpose "to positively impact the financial lives of as many people as possible" to carry forward; please tell people about my fishing expedition... my two books. Thank you.